Studio Thinking

THE REAL BENEFITS OF VISUAL ARTS EDUCATION

LOIS HETLAND,
ELLEN WINNER, SHIRLEY VEENEMA,
AND KIMBERLY M. SHERIDAN

Foreword by David N. Perkins

Teachers College, Columbia University
New York and London

For Elliot Eisner, who blazed the trail.

Published by Teachers College Press, 1234 Amsterdam Avenue, New York, NY 10027

All photos are by Shirley Veenema

Library of Congress Cataloging-in-Publication Data

Studio thinking : the real benefits of visual arts education / Lois Hetland ... [et al.] ; foreword by David N. Perkins.
    p. cm.
  Includes bibliographical references and index.
  ISBN 978-0-8077-4818-3 (pbk. : alk. paper)
    1. Art—Study and teaching—United States. 2. Team learning approach in education—United States.
  I. Hetland, Lois, 1953– II. Teachers College (New York, N.Y.)
  N353.S78 2007
  707.1—dc22   2007019062

ISBN 978-0-8077-4818-3 (paper)

Printed on acid-free paper
Manufactured in the United States of America

14 13 12 11 10 09 08 07   8 7 6 5 4 3 2

Contents

Foreword

You do not have to read very far into *Studio Thinking* to feel that, like Lewis Carroll's Alice, you have stepped through the looking glass into a fantasy world where the colors are brighter, the scenes richer, and the adventure altogether more engaging than what you recall about school. You are likely to find rather drab not only many of your memories of studying mathematics or history, but also many of your school arts experiences. Certainly I do. It's not that my arts teachers lacked the knack; I actually think they were rather good. It's just that not enough time was staked out for the patterns of learning we read about here.

So, having stepped through the looking glass into this strange world of studio learning, how do we make sense of it all? Here the pathways branch. Maybe the visual arts are a special sort of undertaking, some might say. Or maybe these are very special teachers and very special students. Or maybe this is the sort of messing around we can afford when we're not dealing with high-stakes core subject matters.

But what if none of these answers leads anywhere worthwhile? What if, far from a fantasy world, studio learning turns out to be much more realistic regarding the way learning really works than most typical classroom settings?

Toward vetting these possibilities, let's get a little clearer about that studio world on the other side of the looking glass. Exactly what is so very exotic about it, compared to typical patterns of educational practice? My longtime colleagues Lois Hetland, Ellen Winner, Shirley Veenema, and Kim Sheridan do a fine job of portraying the world they have studied, the rhythm and the drama and sometimes the comedy of the studio classroom. For one thing, as the name studio thinking suggests, students spend most of their time developing works of art, instead of reading books or listening to ideas from their arts instructors or doing highly targeted technical exercises. We discover that all these traditional elements have a presence, but with distinctive proportion and placement. We learn that receiving information in the form of Demonstration–Lectures is a strong part of the pattern, but information is immediately applied as the studio work proceeds. It's not just for next week or the year after, it's for today—this canvas, this pot, this sculpture. We also learn that the studio work is spiced with a surprising amount of reflection. The studio teachers we meet are constantly circulating among the learners, prodding them to think about what they are doing and why they are doing it, as well as conducting critical reflective sessions where the group stands back and contemplates the enterprise, its significance, its progress, its shortfalls, and its lessons for the future.

This quick picture of events on the other side of the looking glass leads toward a big generalization. Most educational practice reflects what might be called an *export paradigm*. What learners do today focuses on exporting knowledge for use in a range of envisioned futures. The math in the textbook is for application somewhere, sometime, in some supermarket or on some income tax form or during possible careers in business, engineering, or science. The history acquired might someday help to make sense of an election and to cast a vote more wisely. The specific activities—problem sets for honing skills, answering questions toward understanding principles, memorizing information toward quizzes—are blatantly exercises that target much later payoffs.

What is so very odd about studio learning is its *import paradigm*. It's about using knowledge right now in a serious way for a complex and significant endeavor. Learners deploy what their instructors explain and demonstrate to produce meaningful and engaging works of art. Of course, it's not just about now, it's about later too. The world of later is well served by the kinds of projects addressed and the reflective discourse around them.

Studio learning is not the only pattern of pedagogy that attempts this import paradigm. Many teachers of the core disciplines find ways to engage learners in problem-based learning, project-based learning, case study approaches to learning, and community participation activities, to mention a few. Although such endeavors (like studio learning) can vary enormously in their quality, they display a common deep structure: Students learn for later by importing knowledge into rich undertakings now.

Back to the looking glass question: Where is the fantasy and where is the reality for learning? Well, speaking of looking glasses, it's worth remembering that the whole point of education is to function as a mirror of the future—not a flat mirror, presenting to the learner an anticipated future in all its messy, complicated, and upsetting details, but a convex mirror that renders the future in a substantially reduced and more tractable but still multidimensional form. Learning is likely to be successful to the extent that what learners do today mirrors the future. So the basic point here is pretty simple: An import paradigm in general is a better mirror of the future than an export paradigm, even though, paradoxically, the export paradigm seems to shoot for the future more directly.

Why is the import paradigm a better mirror? Turning to studio thinking specifically, studio activities are fully developed junior versions of what we would like learners to get better at and do more of later. Good studio activities capture the full motivational, technical, and creative dynamic of creating works of art as a professional artist or a serious amateur might do later in life. There are challenges of craft and of expression. There are experiments, failures, and successes. There are demands for reflection and self-discipline. Without the authors' sensitive profile, one might imagine studio work as mostly a matter of developing technical skills. Nothing of the sort. While this is part of the game, the learners' struggles with their challenges cultivate a number of studio habits of mind, for example: persistence, envisioning possibilities, expressing, observing, reflecting, and stretching beyond the immediate and familiar.

The export paradigm does not score so well as a mirror of the future. For one thing, the mirror is often broken into a hundred shards, reflecting only bits and pieces of what will come. The export paradigm suffers from what I like to call "elementitis." We teach the elements now, with the idea that they will coalesce later. We teach component skills, vocabulary, principles, theories, core examples, and when a student asks, "But what is it all for?" the answer promises that it will all come together next year, or in high school, or in college. Mind you, this is not a caution against spending some serious time on technical elements that need targeted development. We see plenty of that in studio work. It's a caution against the endless deferral of large-scale meaningful undertakings.

The export paradigm also tends to suffer from "aboutitis." The export paradigm tries to approach future complexities by talking about them rather than engaging in them. Thus, students typically learn information *about* history—often rather intricate stories about what happened and how others interpreted it—rather than engaging in historical reasoning or interpreting current events through an historical lens. The analogy in the world of art would be learning a lot about artistic creative processes without actually doing much of it. Aboutitis, like elementitis, makes education less of a mirror of the future.

There is a natural reservation about all this. However stimulating our journey through the looking glass of studio learning, perhaps like Lewis Carroll's fantasy worlds it speaks to real life only indirectly and suggestively. Perhaps bits and pieces of studio thinking and other import approaches might fruitfully come into the teaching of the core disciplines, but that's about it. Perhaps those disciplines do not for the most part accommodate so well the rich full-scale endeavors of the studio.

Such a reservation is, I fear, more a failure of ingenuity and imagination than anything else. Indeed, one does not even have to imagine. What amount to studio learning versions of study in the core disciplines already exist in thousands of classrooms, facilitated by thousands of dedicated teachers—various incarnations of strategies mentioned before, such as problem-based learning, project-based learning, case study approaches, community participation, and so on. No fantasies, these are realities today.

And it's no fantasy that, for both logical and psychological reasons, the import paradigm is a better bet. Importing knowledge into complex meaningful endeavors now, with the future in view, is a stronger model of learning than warehousing knowledge for the future. It's the Humpty Dumpty of the export model that's the fragile one. And that's not Jabberwocky! So let's step through the looking glass into *Studio Thinking* and join Lois, Ellen, Shirley, Kim, and a number of art teachers and students for a vision not only of learning in the arts but what could be learning most anywhere.

—David N. Perkins

Preface

It's 10:32 AM, and your art students have just left for their next class. You race into the faculty room for coffee before your next group arrives, only to find visitors from another school who've been looking for you. They want to hear about your classes. How do you teach art, they want to know.

You try to collect your thoughts while attempting to look composed. How can you adequately describe your responsive, intense, multifaceted classroom? There are the students, of course—each one of them is different. And there's the curriculum—you're teaching drawing right now, and painting comes at the end of the term. There's your current project, and the schedule, and how you keep records. There are materials, how you acquire them, store them, maintain them, set up access to them—that's a conversation all by itself. Not to mention dealing with your students' families (it's report time, naturally), the administrators ("Are you covering the standards?"), your fellow art teachers, the partner organizations, the resource room, the social workers, and the school psychologist. Then there's the school principal, always wondering whether time dedicated to the arts might be better used for math or reading. There's what you do about assessment and reporting, and how you deal with teachers in other subjects, and field trips, and homework, and absences. . . .

You ask your visitors, "How much time did you say you had?"

When we began our study of rigorous teaching of visual arts at the high school level, we knew we were entering a complex landscape, and we meant to find language to help teachers and researchers describe it. We were not looking for a prescription that dictated what *should* be done and what was *best*. Rather, we wanted to map visual arts teaching in ways that would allow teachers and researchers to see that territory more clearly, to convey more easily what they knew about classrooms and teaching, to ponder alternate routes they might take, and to learn more readily from other experienced travelers. From the start, we were quite sure that visual arts teaching involves more than instruction in merely art techniques, and we sought to uncover the full spectrum of what re-

ally is taught and how that's accomplished. Our goal was to understand the kinds of thinking that teachers help students develop in visual arts classes and the supports they use to do that.

We have written this book to introduce that descriptive language and to offer practical examples of these two types of concepts—*how* teachers plan and carry out instruction, which we call the *Studio Structures* (see Part I) and *what* is taught in visual arts classes, which we call the *Studio Habits of Mind* (see Part II). The many examples given of art projects are taken from the teachers who graciously invited us into their classes to observe them and their students in action. We provide photographic images, quotations, and anecdotes to ground the concepts in real classrooms within the real opportunities and limits of schools.

We have chosen not to follow the development of each particular art project from start to finish. Rather we draw on parts of a project pertinent to our discussion. The projects are labeled with numbers indicating their chapter and location within a chapter, and for readers who may want to focus on the development of particular projects, we have provided cross references throughout our discussions. In Appendix A we include a table listing all the projects referred to in the book and their locations in the chapters.

Our focus in this book is primarily on the decisions teachers make, but in several places we also show how students respond to these decisions in their work, talk, and behavior. As you read, pay attention to the many ways different teachers describe what they intend students to learn, and the many adaptations each teacher uses of the three organizational studio structures (see Part III). Our aim is to provide strong evidence that the real curriculum in the visual arts extends far beyond the teaching of technique, and to demonstrate that such teaching engenders the development of serious thinking dispositions that are valued both within and beyond the arts.

Before we enter the classroom in Part I, we discuss the background for our work and our goals in Chapter 1. In Chapter 2 we describe the teachers and classes we studied.

Acknowledgments

This research was funded by the J. Paul Getty Trust. We thank Barry Munitz, former President and Chief Executive Officer of the J. Paul Getty Trust, for believing in this project; Jack Meyers, former Deputy Director of the J. Paul Getty Grants program, and Sir Kenneth Robinson, former Senior Advisor to the President of the J. Paul Getty Trust, who served as our program officers; and Deborah Marrow, Director, The Getty Foundation. Patricia Palmer, a researcher at Harvard Project Zero, deserves special thanks for helping with the filming, interviewing, coding, data analysis, and project coordination.

We thank Dr. Linda Nathan, head of the Boston Arts Academy, and Dr. Stephanie Perrin, the now retired head of the Walnut Hill School, for generously allowing us to conduct our research in their schools. This research would not have been possible without the collaboration of five inspiring visual arts teachers, Beth Balliro, Kathleen Marsh, and Guy Michel Telemaque from the Boston Arts Academy, and Jason Green and Jim Woodside from the Walnut Hill school. We also thank the students who allowed us to videotape them as they worked through the long afternoons in the art studio.

Finally, we thank Carol Fromboluti, our program officer at the U.S. Department of Education, which funded an extension of this work in Alameda County, California; Louise Music, Arts Learning Coordinator at the Alameda County Office of Education; Ann Wettrich, Associate Director of the Center for Art and Public Life at the California College of the Arts; and all the teachers and artists who work with us in Alameda County, California. Their efforts affirm our confidence in this work's value for practical use on a daily basis.

ONE

Making the Case for the Arts

WHY ARTS EDUCATION IS NOT JUST A LUXURY

Arts education has always been in a tenuous position in the United States. All too often the arts have been considered a luxury in our schools—an arena for self-expression, perhaps, but not a necessary part of education. This attitude has been exacerbated by the federal No Child Left Behind legislation that was passed in 2001 to improve school performance by setting standards of accountability. With mandated, standardized tests in mathematics, reading, and language arts administered each year, the focus of schools shifted to raising test scores in these areas, since negative consequences resulted for schools if scores did not achieve specified levels. Because No Child Left Behind emphasizes accountability in literacy and numeracy and not the arts, even though the arts are included in the Act as a mandated subject area, the result is even less support now for the arts in many of our schools than there had been in the past.

In reaction to the increasingly weakened position of the arts in our schools, arts advocates have tried to make the case that the arts are important because they improve students' performance in traditional academic subjects that "really count," such as reading and mathematics. Believing that educational decisionmakers won't accept arguments based on the inherent value of arts learning, arts advocates have skirted the fundamental question of the core benefits of studying the arts and fallen back on instrumental justifications for arts education—what we see as possible "bonus" effects of arts education. Few seem to care that these instrumental arguments are made with little empirical or even theoretically plausible basis.

Our position is that before we can make the case for the importance of arts education, we need to find out what the arts actually teach and what art students actually learn. In this book we describe what students are meant to learn when they study the visual arts seriously. We chose the visual arts as our laboratory, but we could as well have chosen music, dance, or drama. It is our hope that others will extend this kind of study to the other art forms. We present the case here that the visual arts teach students not only dispositions that are specific to the visual arts—the craft of the visual arts and an understanding of the larger art world outside of the classroom (Efland, 1976, 1983)—but also at least six dispositions that appear to us to be very general kinds of habits of mind, with the potential to transfer to other areas of learning. The word *disposition* is one we have taken from the work of David Perkins and his colleagues (Perkins, Jay, & Tishman, 1993; Tishman, Jay, & Perkins, 1993; Tishman, Perkins, & Jay, 1995). It refers to a trio of qualities—skills, alertness to opportunities to use these skills, and the inclination to use them—that comprise high-quality thinking. Our Studio Habits of Mind are dispositions that we saw being taught in the studio classrooms; we believe these dispositions are central to artistic thinking and behavior.

Based on our work to date, we cannot yet say whether the dispositions we identified in arts teaching and learning do or do not transfer to other fields. We have not conducted studies to test this possibility. However, the work described here is an important step toward demonstrating transfer from learning in the arts to learning in non-arts disciplines, if and when such transfer occurs. Only when we have established the kinds of dispositions that the arts teach can we then address the questions of whether, to what degree, and in what ways these dispositions are learned and whether they transfer to other areas of the curriculum, including ones considered by some to be more "basic" than the arts.

THE FAILURE OF
INSTRUMENTAL ARGUMENTS

Let's take a look at a few of the most prominent instrumental claims for arts education that have circulated in recent years. A 1995 report by the President's Committee on the Arts and Humanities claimed that "teaching the arts has a significant effect on overall success in school," and noted that both verbal and quantitative SAT scores are higher for high school students who take arts courses than for those who take none (Murfee, 1995, p. 3). In the first few pages of *Champions of Change: The Impact of the Arts on Learning*, an influential publication from the Arts Education Partnership and the President's Committee on the Arts and Humanities, we read that "learners can attain higher levels of achievement through their engagement with the arts" (Fiske, 1999, p. viii). And former Georgia Governor Zell Miller handed out classical music tapes to all parents of newborns, arguing that music improves spatial reasoning and would therefore improve math and engineering skills (cited on "All Things Considered," National Public Radio, January 13, 1998). These are strong claims; and we wondered whether the research evidence supported them.

In a project called REAP (Reviewing Education and the Arts Project), we examined these instrumental justifications for arts education (Winner & Hetland, 2000). We conducted 10 meta-analytic reviews. A meta-analysis combines and averages the results of similar studies to yield a general result. It also compares groups of studies matched by variables that may influence results (e.g., who teaches, the duration of instruction, parental involvement, study design). We combined groups of studies appearing since 1950 that tested the claim that specific forms of arts education result in learning that transfers to specified forms of non-arts learning (e.g., reading, mathematics, verbal/mathematics test scores, spatial reasoning).

Our findings were controversial. They revealed that in most cases there was no demonstrated causal relationship between studying one or more art forms and non-arts cognition. We did, however, find three areas where a causal relationship was conclusively demonstrated:

1. Classroom drama improves reading readiness and reading achievement scores, oral language skills, and story understanding (Podlozny, 2000).
2. Listening to classical music improves performance on some spatial tests in adults. However, since the effect is transitory, lasting only 10–15 minutes, this finding has no direct implications for education (Hetland, 2000a). Unfortunately, people like Zell Miller jumped from this finding to the conclusion that if babies listen to classical music, their SAT scores will show lasting positive effects 18 years later!
3. Classroom music programs in which children experiment with instruments, improvise, and move to music improve performance on some paper and pencil spatial tests (Hetland, 2000b). However, little is known about how long the effect lasts or its relationship to performance in school subjects.

We also reported a number of areas for which no clear causal implications can yet be drawn. We found inconclusive evidence that music improves mathematics learning (Vaughn, 2000) and that dance improves spatial learning (Keinanen, Hetland, & Winner, 2000). We found no evidence that studying visual arts, dance, or music improves reading (Burger & Winner, 2000; Butzlaff, 2000; Keinanen et al., 2000).

That leaves our most controversial finding. We amassed no evidence that studying the arts, either as separate disciplines or infused into the academic curriculum, raises grades in academic subjects or improves performance on standardized verbal and mathematics tests (Winner & Cooper, 2000). This finding was based on an analysis of experimental studies—ones that measured children's academic performance before and after arts training and compared their growth with control groups that did not get as much arts training. Given the studies available in the research literature, our analysis showed that children who studied the arts did no better on achievement tests and earned no higher grades than those who did not study the arts.

This finding has confused many people because there is in fact a correlation in the United States between how much arts students have studied and the level of success they demonstrate on the SAT: SAT scores increase steadily as students take one, two, and three years of arts courses in high school, and they rise more sharply with four years of arts courses (Vaughn & Winner, 2000). But we cannot conclude from this that the arts courses *cause* the scores to rise. The first lesson in any statistics class is not to confuse correlation with causality. There are various other possible explanations for this arts–SAT correlation besides the possibility that studying the arts causes SATs to rise. For example, academically strong students may choose to take more arts courses than academically weak students, because they know that profiles for college admissions are enhanced by demonstrating a wide breadth of interests (here, arts are not causing SAT improvement). Or, parents who value academic achievement in their children may also value the arts and thereby encourage their children to work hard and take arts courses. In this scenario, *parents* are causing both arts involvement and SAT improvement, but the arts play no causal role in SAT scores.

A study in Britain underscores the problems in jumping to a causal conclusion based on this correlational evidence. The British study found just the opposite of what has been reported in the United States—in Britain, the more arts courses students took in secondary school, the *worse* they performed on their national exams (Harland, Kinder, Haynes, & Schagen, 1998)! Of course, researchers in the United Kingdom did not use this as evidence that studying arts *causes* low achievement, because this was not part of their ideology. They realized that in their nation, academically weak students are counseled into the arts, and this is a likely explanation for the negative correlation between arts study and exam scores. The situation is different in the United States: Here we advise weak students to take lower level classes or remedial academic classes, but not to take the arts.

We concluded that the instrumental claims about the effects of arts education on learning in other subjects go far beyond the evidence, a point supported by the Rand report, *Gifts of the Muse: Reframing the Debate About the Benefits of the Arts* (McCarthy, Ondaatje, Zakaras, & Brooks, 2004), and also made in Britain by Adrian Ellis (2003). Anger greeted our report. Some characterized us as enemies of the arts, arguing that publishing our research would destroy quality arts education for children in the United States. One scholar told us that we should

never have asked the question, but having done so, we should have buried our findings.

We were shaken. Our goal had been to find the truth behind the claims, and to change the conversation from glib and superficial arguments for transfer, that in the long run may weaken the case for arts education, to a more thoughtful consideration of what the arts really offer. Arts advocates told us to give up—they called our approach an "arts for arts sake" argument, a tack they insisted was both elitist and doomed to fail. Advocates, they told us, must do what works—and that meant arguing for the arts as a vehicle for strengthening the kinds of basic skills stressed by No Child Left Behind and making this case *whether or not* there was evidence to support it.

Our response? First, justifying the arts only on instrumental grounds will in the end fail, because instrumental claims for the arts are a double-edged sword. If the arts are given a role in our schools because people believe that arts cause academic improvement, then the arts will quickly lose ground if academic improvement does not result, or if the arts prove less effective in improving literacy and numeracy than high-quality, direct instruction in these subjects. When we justify the arts by their secondary, utilitarian value, the arts may prove to have fewer payoffs than academic subjects. Arts educators cannot allow the arts to be justified wholly or primarily in terms of what the arts can do for mathematics or reading. The arts must stand on what they teach directly. If along the way we find that the arts also facilitate academic learning in other subjects, then we have a wonderful side effect. But in justifying arts programs on an instrumental basis, we devalue the arts and fall prey to the anti-arts or arts-as-frills strain that accompanies the back-to-basics movement in the United States.

Second, we have never said that studying the arts does *not* transfer to academic learning. Arts learning may or may not transfer, depending on what is taught and how (Salomon & Perkins, 1989). But the research on transfer to date does not allow us to conclude that transfer of learning occurs. In the words of David Perkins (2001) commenting on the REAP meta-analyses, "it is important to stand back from their findings [about lack of transfer] and ask whether the game is essentially over. . . . Some would say that it had never really begun" (p. 117). We agree with Michael Timpane, former university president and former federal education office policy director, who was paraphrased as follows:

Arts education research today is at an early stage of its development. . . . [in the future, it may become clear that it is similar to] research on reading [a generation ago], where the accumulation of studies over time gradually honed the understanding of educators and policymakers as to the best policies and practices. (Deasy & Fulbright, 2001, p. 34)

The most glaring oversight in the studies conducted thus far on arts transfer is that researchers have failed to document the kinds of thinking that are developed through study of the arts. If the arts are to retain a place within public education, arts educators must answer the questions of what the arts can teach and what students can learn from the arts. Only when we have determined and can document levels of what students actually learn when they study an art form does it make sense to look for transfer of that learning to other subjects. Many of the studies we meta-analyzed did not carefully report what and how teachers were teaching in the arts compared with control classrooms or programs, nor did they assess what students learned. Without knowing how teaching in arts classes differs from teaching in control conditions, nor the level of learning achieved by that arts instruction, one cannot responsibly predict why, what, or how learning in the arts might transfer outside of the arts.

The field of arts education, while passionate, is vague about these questions. So also is the public's understanding of what is learned in the arts. Just ask someone what students learn in art classes, and you are likely to hear that they learn how to paint, or draw, or throw a pot. That's true, but it only tells us what they do, not how they learn to think. This reply is analogous to saying that students learn writing skills in writing class. Of course students learn artistic craft in arts classes. But we must ask what else they learn. Does experience in the arts change students' minds so that they can approach the world as an artist would? Students must be given the opportunity to think like artists, just as they should also be given the opportunity to approach the world mathematically, scientifically, historically, and linguistically. The arts are another way of knowing the world—as important as the other disciplines to our societal health.

THE FRAMEWORK OF STUDIO THINKING

In the study described in this book, we set out to discover what excellent visual art teachers teach, how they teach, and what students learn in their classes. We looked closely at what goes on in five excellent, but very different, arts classrooms. (See Appendix B for details on how we conducted our research.) Despite the debates and the rhetoric about the importance of the arts in education, surprisingly, no other formal studies had, to our knowledge, directly examined the kinds of teaching and learning that actually occur inside the visual arts classroom. A few pioneering studies have investigated in careful detail what goes on in non-arts classrooms (e.g., Lampert's *Teaching Problems and the Problems of Teaching*, 2003; Stigler & Hiebert's *The Teaching Gap*, 1999; and Stevenson's *The Learning Gap*, 1994), and we have followed in the traditions set by these three books.

Based on what we found in our study, we developed the framework we call *Studio Thinking*. This framework describes two aspects of the art classroom: (1) How these classrooms are structured, and here we describe three *studio structures*, and (2) what is taught in these classrooms, and here we describe eight *studio habits of mind*.

Studio Structures

The visual art teachers we studied organized their instruction by using many variations on a few basic patterns of time, space, and interactions. Three of these patterns focus on learning: Demonstration–Lecture, Students-at-Work, and Critique. A fourth focuses on management: Studio Transitions, when students move from one structure to another, or prepare to start or end art class. We included Studio Transitions as a Studio Structure only because, when poorly executed, transitions eat up valuable learning time, and when well-run, they may also provide a few more moments for focused, one-on-one interactions between teacher and students. An overview of the three learning structures is presented in Figure 1.1, and they are discussed in more detail in Chapter 4.

Studio Habits of Mind

We also observed a "hidden curriculum" in visual arts classes, and we argue that this is their real curriculum. We came to the conclusion that, in addition to two basic arenas of learning—teaching the craft of the visual arts (e.g., techniques, tool use), and teaching about the art world beyond the classroom (e.g., art history, visual culture, the world of

Figure 1.1. Three Studio Structures

Demonstration–Lectures

- Teachers (and others) deliver information about processes and products and set assignments
- Information is immediately useful to students for class work or homework
- Information is conveyed quickly and efficiently to reserve time for work and reflection
- Visual examples are frequent and sometimes extended
- Interaction occurs to varying degrees

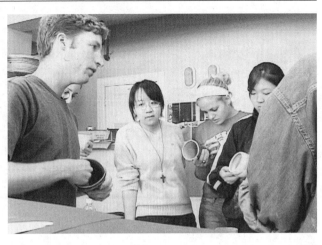

Students-at-Work

- Students make artworks based on teachers' assignments
- Assignments specify materials, tools, and/or challenges
- Teachers observe and consult with individuals or small groups
- Teachers sometimes talk briefly to the whole class

Critique

- Central structure for discussion and reflection
- A pause to focus on observation, conversation, and reflection
- Focus on student works
- Works are completed or in progress
- Display is temporary and informal

galleries, curators, critics), at least six other important kinds of general cognitive and attitudinal dispositions are developed in serious visual arts classes. These dispositions are central to learning in many subjects, and they may well transfer to academic subjects.

The dispositions that emerged from our study bear some striking similarities to those that Elliot Eisner, in his book *The Arts and the Creation of Mind* (2002), has argued that the arts teach (e.g., learning to attend to relationships, flexibility, and the ability to shift direction, expression, and imagination).

Our research sets the stage for informed studies of the transfer of arts learning. However, whether or not transfer of learning occurs from arts instruction, the kinds of thinking developed by the arts are important in and of themselves, as important as the thinking developed in more traditionally academic subjects.

In our study we witnessed teachers striving to instill all eight "Studio Habits of Mind" (or dispositions). We observed that whenever teachers were helping students develop technical skills (the habit of mind we refer to as Develop Craft: Technique and

Figure 1.2. Eight Studio Habits of Mind

Develop Craft

Technique: Learning to use tools (e.g., viewfinders, brushes), materials (e.g., charcoal, paint); Learning artistic conventions (e.g., perspective, color mixing)
Studio Practice: Learning to care for tools, materials, and space

Engage and Persist

Learning to embrace problems of relevance within the art world and/or of personal importance, to develop focus and other mental states conducive to working and persevering at art tasks

Envision

Learning to picture mentally what cannot be directly observed and imagine possible next steps in making a piece

Express

Learning to create works that convey an idea, a feeling, or a personal meaning

Observe

Learning to attend to visual contexts more closely than ordinary "looking" requires, and thereby to see things that otherwise might not be seen

Reflect

Question and Explain: Learning to think and talk with others about an aspect of one's work or working process
Evaluate: Learning to judge one's own work and working process, and the work of others in relation to standards of the field

Stretch and Explore

Learning to reach beyond one's capacities, to explore playfully without a preconceived plan, and to embrace the opportunity to learn from mistakes and accidents

Understand Art World

Domain: Learning about art history and current practice
Communities: Learning to interact as an artist with other artists (i.e., in classrooms, in local arts organizations, and across the art field) and within the broader society

Studio Practice), they were also inculcating one or more of the other seven habits of mind. These habits of mind are dispositions that are used in many academic arenas and in daily life: the dispositions of *Observation, Envisioning, Reflecting, Expressing, Exploring, Engaging and Persisting*, and *Understanding the Art World*. Once taught in the arts studio, these dispositions might transfer to other contexts of learning. (An overview of the Studio Habits of Mind is presented in Figure 1.2, and they are discussed in detail in the chapters in Part II.)

These habits of mind are important not only for the visual arts but for all the arts disciplines, as well as for many other kinds of study. Similar mental habits are deployed in the serious study of dance, music, theater, science, mathematics, history, literature, and writing. For example, students must learn a great deal about tools and materials in a science lab, and this kind of learning is analogous to the art studio habit we call *Develop Craft*. The disposition to *Engage and Persist* is clearly important in any serious endeavor: Students need to learn to find problems of interest and work with them deeply over sustained periods of time. The disposition *Envision* is important in the sciences (e.g., generating hypotheses), in history (e.g., developing historical imagination), and in mathematics (e.g., imagining how to represent space and time algorithmically). *Express* is important in any kind of writing that one does, even in analytical nonfiction and historical narratives. *Observe*, or its corollaries, listen and attend, is required across all disciplines. The disposition to *Reflect* (becoming aware of one's decisions and working style, becoming able to assess one's work and that of others) is also important in any discipline. Similarly, *Stretch and Explore* emphasizes the need to experiment and take risks, regardless of the domain of focus. *Understand the Art World* has its parallels in other disciplines, in which students are asked to identify links between what they do as *students* in a particular domain and what *professionals* in that domain do, have done, and are doing. Good science, history, English, and mathematics teachers (as well as teachers of any other subject) propose problems to think about that are currently being grappled with by contemporary practitioners and engage their students in understanding how the work and thinking taught in classes operate in the world beyond the classroom.

However, we urge our readers to be cautious in interpreting these comments. Just because a habit learned in the arts is also used in other disciplines, it does not follow that learning one of these habits

in the arts classroom actually strengthens that habit when the student enters a science, mathematics, history, literature, or writing classroom. It may work the other way around, with habits learned in academic subjects transferring to learning in the arts. Alternatively, the same habits could be learned separately in each kind of classroom. To do so, however, explicit efforts to link subjects must be made regularly if transfer is to occur reliably (Salomon & Perkins, 1989). The transfer from arts to academics hypothesis remains just that—a hypothesis to be tested. But with these studio habits identified, we can now test plausible hypotheses.

For example, it seems reasonable to suggest that the habits of both observing and envisioning may transfer to a science class. If students were explicitly taught to think about habits of mind that they had acquired in arts class and to try to use them in biology class, for example, these dispositions might indeed transfer. In short, for each of the habits identified as learned in the arts, we can now think carefully about how and where this habit might be deployed outside of the arts and then test for such transfer. The first step is to assess how well each habit has been learned in a parent domain (art is the "parent" if learning transfers from art to another subject); the second step is to determine whether the strength with which a habit in the arts is learned predicts how well the habit is used in a target domain, outside of the arts (e.g., mathematics or reading). This is a logical way to go about testing for transfer.

The model we present here of visual arts learning is consistent with, but does not replace, the National Standards for Arts Education (from the Consortium of National Art Education Associations) or the many state standards that have been developed for learning in the arts. The standards specify a particular group's stance (e.g., a state or a national arts association) about particular levels and types of student achievement in the visual arts. In contrast, our Studio Habits of Mind identify more general cognitive and attitudinal dispositions that allow students to meet these standards. Thus our findings complement the standards and allow us to unify learning in the visual arts from the earliest to the most advanced levels of education, and across national and local contexts.

CONCLUSION

There are promising signs emerging today in arts education that the role of arts learning in and out of schools may be growing stronger. California recently reinstituted state-wide support for arts in public schools with $105 million in funds designated in 2006 and intended to be reallocated annually, along with a $500-million, one-time allocation to build infrastructure for the arts and physical education (e.g., buying kilns, presses, computer arts equipment). Parents want their children to be inspired and not just memorize facts, and they are coming to realize that the arts play a critical role in inspiring children (Bostrom, 2003). The Wallace Foundation funded the Rand Corporation's report that argues against instrumental claims for the arts (McCarthy et al., 2004) and has commissioned a report by Harvard Project Zero on what counts as quality in arts education today. And there is renewed interest among private funders in establishing what the arts in themselves do (the Dana, Ford, and Hewlett Foundations are currently funding such initiatives).

We hope that this book provides arts educators, advocates, and researchers with some arguments they need to lobby for strengthening the arts in our schools. Arts teachers, those who prepare arts teachers for licensure, and principals and curriculum directors can use our findings in conversation with one another, with beginning teachers, and with teachers of other disciplines, so that the understanding of arts' role in teaching disciplinary thinking becomes clearer to all educators. Our findings should help art teachers refine their teaching practices, help arts advocates explain arts education to decisionmakers, and help researchers explain proposed studies to funders. Non-arts teachers have much to learn from how excellent arts teachers personalize instruction, engage in just-in-time interventions as they circle the room while students work, and stimulate students' critical and self-reflective skills during regular critique sessions. Finally, the Studio Thinking Framework lays the foundation for more precisely targeted and plausible transfer studies.

TWO

Taking Arts Education Seriously

OUR SCHOOL-BASED COLLEAGUES

In the first chapter, we explained why we undertook the work presented in this book. Our goal was to identify "what" is taught in visual arts (eight dispositions we call the *Studio Habits of Mind*) and "how" teachers do that (organizing classroom time, space, and interactions using three *Studio Structures*). In this chapter we introduce the two schools and five teachers with whom we worked to identify the complexities of teaching and learning in the visual arts.

In launching our research project, we looked for schools in the Boston area that took the arts seriously. By "seriously," we meant that they explicitly defined themselves as dedicated to the arts; they hired teachers who were practicing artists; they admitted students selectively, considering students' portfolios; and their programs included intensive arts instruction. We chose the Boston Arts Academy, a public, urban pilot school, and the Walnut Hill School, an independent residential school outside of Boston. At these schools, students receive over 10 hours of arts instruction per week. Classes at the Boston Arts Academy contain about 25 students; those at Walnut Hill, about 15 students.

Five teachers, three at Boston Arts Academy and two at Walnut Hill, agreed to collaborate with us in our study of visual arts teaching. These five teachers were selected by the heads of each school as excellent teachers who might be interested in allowing us to study their classrooms. We then approached each teacher and discussed our project; each teacher willingly agreed to work with us. Not only did they make it possible for us to videotape one of their classes every month throughout the academic year, but they also granted us lengthy interviews following each class, and these interviews often lasted 2 hours.

THE THREE
BOSTON ARTS ACADEMY TEACHERS

Beth Balliro: Painting and Ceramics

Beth Balliro (see Figure 2.1) has worked as an artist/educator with Boston youth for over 10 years and at the Boston Arts Academy since its opening in 1998. She has taught visual arts and music, supervised teen mural projects, and directed public performances in conjunction with national initiatives against youth violence.

Figure 2.1. Beth Balliro with student

Beth sees teaching art as very political. She believes strongly that urban students need to learn to speak about their art in the world, and she feels that the Boston Arts Academy will have failed if its students buy into the "disenfranchised artist" myth. She sees that myth as furthering the isolation and frustration of urban students, which ultimately leads to their stopping the making of art. She sees her students as artists, and she wants to help them take on the challenge and responsibility of being artists who are heard. "That's a greater challenge than even making art for most people." Art makes a society a place worth living in, says Beth, so urban students have to figure out how to demand that they be heard, using the language of the society to make their point.

We filmed five of Beth's 9th-grade classes in a course she describes as "two-thirds clay and one-third painting." Twenty-seven students were enrolled in this class, which met on Monday and Wednesday afternoons from 1:00 to 3:30 PM from February through June.

Beth is a nationally exhibited painter in the *plein air* tradition and her recent work, which documents active wildfires, can be found on the cover of *Salamander Magazine*'s 2003 edition. In addition, she is the 2003 Isabella Stewart Gardner Museum's Teacher-in-Residence and teaches at the Massachusetts College of Art.

Beth earned a Bachelor of Arts degree cum laude from Smith College and a Master of Science in Art Education and professional licensure in Massachusetts from the Massachusetts College of Art. In the summer of 2001, immediately prior to her participation in this research, she was awarded a fellowship from the Surdna Foundation and studied ceramics in Japan.

Kathleen Marsh: Sculpture and Drawing

Kathleen Marsh (see Figure 2.2) is a founding faculty member of the Boston Arts Academy and has been teaching there since 1998. She strives to instill in her students the foundational skill of rigorous habits of work. She believes in the importance of observational drawing as a way to teach students how to see. She wants her students to learn that looking and drawing are closely intertwined and that looking connects to thinking and interpretation. She uses assessment as a learning tool, giving students explicit criteria for what counts as distinguished performance for each project (scoring rubrics). She encourages self- and peer-critique and -assessment, and stresses the importance of affirming students' strengths even as she breaks down their set conceptions of drawing.

She explains that her students arrive "with this sort of focused way of looking . . . and they have this set way of making art . . . and it's our job to crack that open and say, OK. This is great—what you've done so far, but look at all this other stuff you could do." Kathleen thinks in terms of a 4-year sequence from 9th to 12th grade. Foundational habits of working, thinking, and seeing are begun in the 9th grade and are continually revisited and strengthened over the students' 4 years at the school. She has found that

if habits of work are ingrained early, she can be less explicit about the need for these habits later on, as students begin to focus on higher and more personalized artistic goals.

Figure 2.2. Kathleen Marsh in the classroom

We filmed nine of Kathleen's classes, four 9th-grade and five 12th-grade sessions. Twenty-seven students were enrolled in the 9th-grade class, which met Monday and Wednesday afternoons from 1:00 to 3:30 PM, September through January. Nineteen students were enrolled in the 12th-grade class, which met second semester from February through June on Tuesday and Thursday mornings from 9:00 to 11:30 AM.

Prior to the Boston Arts Academy, Kathleen taught for 10 years in the Boston, Somerville, and Georgetown school districts; at Massachusetts College of Art and Wheelock College; and in out-of-school programs, such as Arts in Progress and the Museum of Fine Arts, and was the coordinator for an arts-based after-school program for 3 years.

Kathleen, after studying voice at the Eastman School of Music, received her B.F.A. in sculpture from Syracuse University in 1983, where she was a Wirt-Newman scholar, and her Master of Science in Art Education with professional licensure from the Massachusetts College of Art in 1996, where she received the Hugh Sloan Award for distinguished teaching. She has exhibited her work locally and nationally and has been affiliated with several local projects, including First Night, Federated Dorchester Neighborhood Houses, and Worcester Art All-State.

Guy Michel Telemaque: Photography and Design

Guy Michel (Mickey) Telemaque (see Figure 2.3) has taught at the Boston Arts Academy since 2000. Like Kathleen, Mickey believes in the importance of teaching his students to see anew. He wants them to forget what they know and how they think the world looks and see the world with fresh eyes. He urges students to experiment and to use their earlier drafts as source material for later work. He stresses process over product, so that students will not get blocked by the desire to make perfect pieces right away. He wants students to develop design skills that become second nature to them—like waking up in the morning or tying their shoelaces. He stresses the basics of design. When students enter the 9th grade, he tells us that "it's not about feelings now. I'm not trying to get them to emote on a page. At this point, composition should be about space, and line, and form." He strives to instill a serious work ethic in his students.

Figure 2.3. Mickey Telemaque talks to his class

We filmed eight of Mickey's classes, six in 9th-grade design and two in photography (10th and 11th grades). Thirteen students were enrolled in this class each term (fall and spring), which met on Tuesday and Thursday afternoons from 2:00 to 3:30 PM. The photography classes had 11 students each. Tenth grade met on Monday afternoons from 2:00 to 3:30 PM, and 11th met on Tuesday mornings from 9:00 to 11:30 AM.

Mickey was born in Queens, New York, and grew up in Miami, Florida. He received his B.A. in Fine Arts from Flagler College in 1992 and his M.F.A. in photography from the Massachusetts College of Art in 1998. Mickey taught for a year at the Southeast Museum of Photography, and at the Massachusetts College of Art before coming to the Boston Arts Academy. His work has been exhibited in several galleries and collected by the Southeast Museum of Photography.

THE TWO WALNUT HILL TEACHERS

Jason Green: Ceramics and Ceramic Sculpture

Jason Green (see Figure 2.4) began teaching at Walnut Hill after graduating with his M.F.A. from the New York State College of Ceramics at Alfred

University in 1998. Jason stresses the importance of getting students to stretch, to take risks, and to experiment. "I think it's important as artists that we are always expanding and exploring the medium, and because of that, I try to get a lot of students to innovate . . . develop ways of learning that aren't expected." His teaching combines the inculcation of basic skills with the assignment of projects that encourage a great deal of choice, freedom, and experimentation. He sees technical knowledge as liberating: Without technical knowledge, "there's not really a chance for discussion about choices." Jason teaches ceramics, and his vision of ceramics is a broad one. He tells his students that making things on the wheel is a form of drawing, that clay is a receptive material that records mark-making actions just like paper records the marks we make with pen.

We filmed eight of Jason's classes in his ceramic sculpture class. The fall term focused on wheel-throwing, and the spring term on hand-building. Ten students were enrolled in this class, which met on Tuesday afternoons from 2:00 to 5:00 PM.

Figure 2.4. Jason Green consults with a student

As a ceramic sculptor, Jason uses brick, tile, and other fabricated architectural elements combined with decorative interior surfaces. His patterned terra cotta fragments investigate the relationships between physical spaces, the body, time, and memory. He was awarded an Emerging Artist Grant from the American Craft Council in 2003, and in 2005 received an Individual Artist Grant from the Massachusetts Cultural Council. Recent exhibitions include the Invitational Exhibit of International Ceramics at the Guangdong Shiwan Ceramic Museum in China, Tiles on the Edge at Pewabic Pottery in Detroit, Mastery in Clay at the Clay Studio in Philadelphia, and Ceramic Artists of the Northeast at the Slater Museum in Norwich, Connecticut. His work can be seen at http://www.absolutearts.com/portfolios/j/jasongreen.

Jim Woodside: Drawing

Jim Woodside (see Figure 2.5) has been a teacher and the Director of Visual Art at Walnut Hill since 1988. Jim views drawing as a language that, if well taught, becomes a fluid tool rather than a mechanistic application of rules. He tries to demystify art-making, telling his students that making art is just a normal form of "work." He connects art to life, telling his students that if their artwork is not connected to their lives and their selves, then their artwork will lack meaning. He creates a studio atmosphere in his class where students learn from their peers as they watch one another work and as they participate in daily critiques discussing one another's works.

We filmed nine of Jim's classes. Eight of the visits were to his drawing class. Fourteen students were enrolled in this class, which met on Wednesday afternoons from 2:00 to 5:00 PM. The ninth class was his Senior Studio, a critique class of twelve seniors that met on Friday afternoons from 2:00 to 4:00 PM.

Figure 2.5. Jim Woodside leading a critique

Jim is a landscape painter who has exhibited his work regularly throughout the northeast United States for over 20 years. A 2003 grantee from the National Science Foundation's Artists and Writers Program, he traveled to Antarctica to paint landscapes. Upon his return, he exhibited this work at the Tatistcheff Gallery in New York City, and he has lectured extensively on his "Painting in Antarctica" experience. These lecture venues have ranged from the U.S. Environmental Protection Agency "Science Seminar Series" to pre-school classrooms.

Jim received his M.F.A. degree in 1983 from the Maryland Institute College of Art, Hoffberger School of Painting. Prior to that, he participated in the Independent Study Program at the Whitney Museum of American Art.

CONCLUSION

We chose the schools we did because we wanted to find out what can happen in the art room under the best of circumstances—when the teachers are themselves artists, when the students are serious about studying art, and where extensive time is spent studying art every day. Of course, these are not the typical conditions for the teaching of art. But we reasoned that it makes sense to observe teachers in schools in which they have the authority, time, and resources to make and act on professional art-education decisions.

Since we only filmed one class per month taught by each teacher, we had to make sure that we were not missing anything. We believe that what we saw was representative of what went on in our five teachers' classrooms. We interviewed each teacher prior to the study about his or her teaching philosophy and goals for the entire semester's class. In addition, we interviewed each teacher subsequent to taping each class: We showed them clips from the class, asked them about their intentions behind their interventions, and asked them to identify evidence for their assertions in depth. We also showed our manuscript to each of the teachers, asking them for a "validity check" to see whether we missed anything important about their teaching. All five of them told us that they felt we had captured the heart of their teaching. We have presented this work to a wide range of audiences around the world. No one has identified an artistic habit of mind that we cannot readily categorize as one of our eight habits.

We stress that the art classes we present here are not unique. True, we worked in very unusual schools, ones that grant extensive time to the arts to students who have chosen to focus on the arts. Nonetheless, the actual methods used by the teachers, and the projects students worked on, are ones that art teachers use in all kinds of classrooms in all kinds of schools. Thus, the model we present can guide planning and instruction in most visual arts classrooms. The model we present is the real, if sometimes hidden, curriculum in the visual arts classroom.

Part I

STUDIO CLASSROOMS:
THE *HOW* OF STUDIO TEACHING

Walk into a studio art class, and you may feel you have left school. The students look relaxed; sometimes they sit on the floor or music plays softly. After materials are set up students dig in, not concerned about getting clay on their hands or paint on their jeans. You see the teacher introducing concepts and demonstrating, and then you watch as students become engrossed in the day's project. Often their work is part of a much longer project, already begun, extending for weeks. Sometimes a work of art by an established artist is displayed and discussed because something the artist did relates to today's work. Today we are working on light. Let's see how Edward Hopper used light. Today we are working on portraits. Let's look at Cubist portraits and compare them with more realistic ones to get a feel for the many ways there are to represent the world.

Students talk among themselves quietly as they begin to work, and the teacher circles around, watching for teachable moments and zeroing in on individual students with a comment, suggestion, question, or critique. At the end of class there is often a critique in which students gather to share and discuss their work, a session in which critical judgment and metacognition are nurtured.

A studio classroom is much more complicated than it looks at first impression. The students who originally appeared so casual are actually working hard—they are thinking visually, analytically, critically, creatively. In Chapter 3 we discuss how teachers develop a studio culture—how they design the physical environment, how they create projects that are engaging and focused on developing students' thinking. In Chapter 4 we delve into the three structures of a studio art classroom through which teachers guide student learning: Demonstration–Lecture, Students-at-Work, and Critique.

THREE

Elements of
Studio Classrooms

On the surface, a studio classroom might appear to require little teacher planning. Teachers usually talk briefly and often quite informally. While students are making art, teachers might appear, to casual observation, to be milling about aimlessly. And when the group looks at students' work and talks about it together, teachers respond in an impromptu way and encourage students to do much of the reflecting. Getting students to clean everything up might appear to be the toughest part of art teaching!

However, this informality belies the careful thinking and artfulness required to make a studio class work. As we observed art teachers, we saw three areas of focus that teachers used to make their art classrooms into places in which students engage rigorously in learning:

- Creating a studio culture
- Focusing thinking with studio assignments
- Teaching through artworks

In what follows, we describe the elements we observed in each of these areas of focus.

CREATING A STUDIO CULTURE

Studio classrooms have a different "feel" than classrooms in many other disciplines. The space is set up to promote work-flow, there is sometimes music playing to create a mood and to sustain and/or modulate students' energy, and students are usually absorbed by handling (often messy and sometimes complex and even dangerous) materials and tools.

The teachers we observed were attentive to a range of elements (e.g., space, time, language, music, and routines) that contributed to creating a studio culture to support the learning they intended.

Designing the Physical Space

The arrangement of space is a powerful factor in helping to accomplish instructional goals. A primary consideration is getting materials and tools into students' hands efficiently. When teachers have the space, they often set up materials stations that students can access from several directions to avoid waiting, and ask students to collect what they need. Other times, when materials must be put away because space is shared, teachers use student assistants to pass out materials from a central materials center. Teachers sometimes choose to set up the classroom just enough to get students started, and then, throughout the class, bring students new materials for later phases of work.

Wall space is also a potential teaching tool. At the Boston Arts Academy, Kathleen, Beth, and Mickey organized wall spaces, for example, to express disciplinary, school, and personal values; models of work; and intentions for learning. Even though the rooms at the Academy are shared, teachers still use the walls to display a rich array of professional and student artworks and texts of various types, including instructions for routines, goals, quotations, announcements, and humorous and personal reminders. Similarly, at Walnut Hill, Jason and Jim also use the walls to teach. One wall in Jason's ceramic studio features a large matrix of tiles that reveals how systematic mixing and layering of glazes produce different effects after firing. Jim's classroom walls are usually lined with students' works in progress, both from students in the current class and from students in other classes.

The organization and labeling of space to house materials and tools is also an important consideration. Jason has clear plastic drawers labeled and filled with ceramic tools, and he labels shelves with students' names as personal storage areas for works in progress. Jim labels spaces for student portfolios, again, so all student work is accessible to both students and teacher for review and reflection.

Configurations of furniture also have a great impact on how classes function. Beth sets up the studio in a totally different arrangement when she starts a unit on clay, and she switches it again when she starts a painting unit. These adjustments accommodate different social groupings as well as different uses of materials. Jason also reconfigures the classroom space between units, removing the pottery wheels when the class begins to focus on sculpture. As sculpture begins, he sets up a central table and individual sculpture stools so students can choose how to position themselves relative to their work and their peers. Jim keeps his studio quite open, often with a central object of focus (e.g., a 10-foot diameter still life of variously sized boxes, a splay of crumpled black paper hanging from the ceiling). This spatial choice unifies the class and also encourages students to explore several vantage points before committing to a position for drawing. In addition, Jim uses three different "seating" options to promote students' taking varied perspectives on their work. Students can observe from a low level (sitting on the floor with a drawing board propped on a brick), from a midlevel (sitting astride drawing horses), or from above (standing at easels). All of these space considerations build in flexibility that reminds and encourages students to think about the effects of other people, materials, and processes on the concepts being addressed. Teachers use space to support their learning intentions.

Designing Classroom Light and Sound

Teachers also create atmospheres with light and sound to help students persist in their work. In several of the classes we observed, teachers used music as background to help students develop a flow in their work, whether to energize or calm them. For example, both Kathleen and Mickey sometimes held "Open Studio," in which students harness their energy with popular music and a social buzz. In these classes, students joke, talk, and move around a lot as they work. Jim often plays more upbeat music in the late afternoons, to lift the energy during the late hours of long afternoon classes when students are tired. And for clean-up, some teachers use popular music to provide an energetic, upbeat atmosphere and to manage the routine—when the song is over, the class assesses what's left to be cleaned and starts in again as necessary.

Conversely, for projects that require quiet concentration, Kathleen sometimes declares a "Closed Studio." In these sessions, students work silently while calming music plays in the background as an aid to concentration for those who are easily distracted. Jim often used more complex jazz playing quietly in the early hours of classes, when students are making decisions about composition and focusing on new skills. Again, teachers make the choice of music intentionally so that it supports students' learning for particular challenges.

Light is another tool teachers use to set atmospheres conducive to learning. In Kathleen's portrait assignment, students each set an individual light source to create the strong values they were emphasizing in their charcoal drawings. Jim frequently changes the lighting for particular challenges and even during a single class. He pulls the shades, uses spotlights, turns overhead lights on or off, and occasionally lines the window shades with strings of small white lights. In addition to creating aesthetic interest, such variation emphasizes the strong influence of light on mood and encourages students to use it as an element in their artworks to express different attitudes and meanings with values.

Designing the Social Climate

Teachers not only design the physical space, they also design informal and sometimes more formal ways that students interact with one another and with teachers to create a social climate that nurtures learning.

Teacher–Student Interactions. As students make artworks, teachers observe and intervene. Such observation and responsive teaching is critical to student learning. Teachers are also aware and thoughtful, however, of students' needs for privacy at times to develop a relationship with materials, tools, and their own work. For instance, Jim often spends the first 10 or so minutes of a Students-at-Work session tidying up and organizing the classroom. That is not just an efficient use of time for managing materials. It also gives the students a chance to enter into their work in personally meaningful ways. Similarly, we noticed Jason working on his own coil sculpture during a Coil Project. He used his sculpture stool as a perch from which to observe students when they needed time without being distracted. By stepping back, these teachers set an atmosphere of unobserved independence for the students, while remaining close enough to see what is going on and being ready to intervene with questions, suggestions, or demonstrations as the need and opportunity arise.

Studio teachers' use of language models artful talk for students that helps them think about their work in more sophisticated ways. The language also conveys important messages about what is valued and possible in that classroom. The teachers we observed often used such words and phrases as *decisions, planning, think about, what if, you might consider, I wonder if, experiment, it might be because, you could try (x or y or z)*, and so forth, all of which are utterances intended to encourage approaching work or ideas thoughtfully. This kind of talk encourages the studio habits of Reflection (*describe it*), Envision (*think about it*), and Stretch and Explore (*experiment*). Students internalize the vocabularies for thinking about art that teachers model. In our observations of classes and our later interviews with students, we frequently heard students use the same language as their teachers when talking about their work.

Peer Interactions. Teachers also need to ensure that students feel safe and respected by each other. For instance, teachers at the Boston Arts Academy explicitly instruct students in how to make constructive criticism rather than hurtful comments in critiques. For the beginning students, they taught peer critique methods such as making a positive comment first and then phrasing suggestions for improvement in neutral terms (e.g., "I wonder what would happen if you . . . ," "Have you thought about trying . . . ," "That makes me think about . . . ," and "I had trouble with that in [x assignment] and I tried . . . and it worked pretty well.").

Teachers also want to create a climate where students are engaged with each other, collaborating and learning to participate in a community of artists. While Jim acknowledges that students are not always as clear and helpful to each other in their advice during critiques as he might be, he

encourages them to talk so that they learn to learn from one another:

> If I had them never talking to each other . . . it could be a sort of a flat atmosphere where not much exchange goes on. At worst, it could be a competitive, threatening atmosphere . . . you're going to have an atmosphere. . . . Something's going to happen, so you may as well take control of it and make it serve your needs, serve the class.

FOCUSING THINKING WITH STUDIO ASSIGNMENTS

Assignments are one of the main ways that teachers guide and nurture students' learning. By constraining a few directions of thinking and emphasizing others, assignments can shape the direction students aim their investigations with materials, tools, and processes.

What Are Studio Assignments?

Assignments guide particular kinds of learning. They specify or suggest the range of materials and tools to be used, and they pose one or more challenges that are open-ended and result in varied solutions. Assignments vary in length (from a few minutes to several weeks), can be done in class or as homework, and promote growth for students at a wide range of levels. Most centrally, assignments focus students on particular intentions teachers have for their learning.

How Assignments Support Different Dispositions

A "dispositional" perspective (Perkins, Jay, & Tishman, 1993) is useful in considering the potential of assignments relative to learning. Such a view emphasizes how teachers might encourage students' development of artistic abilities, the inclination to use these abilities, and an alertness to opportunities for employing these abilities.

Ability. Often called "skill," ability in a studio context involves controlling materials, tools, and processes such that intentions can be realized. But there are subtler skills, too, that involve students in learning to handle verbal and visual information, plan artworks and processes, make decisions about taking risks and addressing errors, and manage mental and emotional states to enhance their capacities to continue working.

An assignment "works" when it guides students at diverse skill levels to develop one or more habits that are just at the edge of their skill, so that their efforts advance their disciplinary understanding. For instance, when Beth taught color theory, she introduced the color wheel (see Examples 5.1 and 7.1). Students copied the wheel and a few notes into their journals. Then they made paintings that required them to use color to express an environment in which an imaginary creature—a creature they had imagined that symbolized aspects of themselves—was born (using complementary colors) and died (using neutral colors). Some students in the class were skilled in the use of color and some had never thought about color theoretically before. But this assignment allowed students to enter from any level of learning and build their skills through exploration and reflection.

Inclination. Ability is only of value when it is put to use. Inclination refers to a person's motivation to apply various mental and physical skills. Inclination can be extrinsically motivated (i.e., work completed for a grade, to please someone, to fulfill a requirement), intrinsically motivated (i.e., work completed to discover an answer or a new question, or to satisfy curiosity), or can combine external and internal motivations (Amabile, 1996). An effective assignment challenges students to put skills to use in new contexts that engage them in the process of making–perceiving–reflecting (Winner & Simmons, 1992). In great assignments, extrinsic motivation begins to take its rightful backseat to intrinsic motivation, which develops as students engage in genuine inquiry and creation.

For example, Jim asks students to use the drawing skills developed through a year of instruction (e.g., composition, value, figure drawing, quality of line) to make cubist drawings. As he explained to his students (see Example 12.4), in cubism, objects are depicted in all three dimensions, not by means of two- and three-point perspective, but by showing multiple and conflicting views of an object simultaneously. Jim had students make cubist drawings by posing a student on a swivel chair that he turned every 10 minutes to face another direction. Students were to superimpose the several views of the model in one drawing. Students struggled with this new way of drawing, while Jim showed individuals examples from Picasso, Braque, and others who

had approached the challenge of depicting three-dimensional reality on a flat surface. "I want to do that," a student said, as Jim showed her a cubist work. She did not want to do it just because it was an assignment, but because she enjoyed the challenge. For this student at least, Jim had succeeded in creating intrinsic motivation for the assignment. She was *inclined* to use her drawing skills in pursuit of making a cubist drawing.

Alertness. "Attention, attention, attention" says the Zen master. Skill and inclination require only one further element for a student to grow in expertise. That element is alertness. Where, in the stream of life's experiences, can we recognize opportunities to use abilities to good advantage? Alertness is that recognition. Once an opportunity is recognized, ability and inclination can be put to work purposefully.

For example, Beth assigned students to "spy" on their families to see how they used "vessels" at home, which supported their *alertness* to consider the functions of vessels. Kathleen assigned a texture collection to be made by rubbing patterns found outside and in students' homes—again, enhancing their alertness to an aesthetic element she wanted them to begin using more mindfully in their work. Similarly, Mickey asked students to cut thumbnail images from popular magazines such that the objects and people became unrecognizable as images and transformed into pure design elements—alerting students to the presence of design elements in familiar contexts. Jason asked students to drink from their own fired ceramic cups so that they would develop awareness of nonfunctional elements such as sharp lips and awkward handles. All of these assignments help students develop habits of alertness to aesthetic qualities in the world around them.

An assignment succeeds in developing alertness to the extent that it helps students notice connections between their subjective experience and the world around them, guiding them to think about their experiences as visual artists do. Assignments have to be sufficiently focused to direct students' attention toward ideas valued by professionals who take visual art seriously. Assignments that address central ideas in the field of visual art provide such opportunities by offering windows into what experts consider and work with when they create and appreciate art. For example, sessions focusing on cubism, or on perspective, or on value lend themselves to this kind of learning. At the same time, assignments need to be roomy enough to leave plenty of space for the individual's intentions (e.g., creating a portrait of himor herself as an animal in an environment) and passions (e.g., at the end of a long afternoon class, Jim asks students to fill in spaces in perspective drawings with patterns that are personally evocative for them). Thus, a well-balanced assignment both channels and awakens perception, and in these ways, supports the development of alertness.

TEACHING THROUGH ARTWORKS

In many high school classes in non-arts disciplines, connections between work made by professionals and by students are often left to chance. Professional work seems more a source of "true facts" than of evidence for how disciplinary experts think and express that thinking. Nor is student work exploited as a way to foster thinking, or as a way to show the thinking that students have already developed. Instead, work is completed in private, graded in private, and privately stowed (or thrown) away.

In contrast, in the studio classes we observed, work by both professionals and students has a prominent place as evidence of thinking and understanding. Whether as an introduction to an assignment, a quick example while students are making art, or when teachers and students are talking about work in progress or completed, studio teachers seize frequent opportunities to use works of art as sources of information. Because "making" is at the center of the studio experience, what is made also has an important place. Artwork, both finished and in progress, is made by professionals and made by students, and we saw teachers employ a number of strategies to make the artwork into effective teaching tools.

Student work is public, and teachers use it as a central tool for learning and reflection. Often, student work from various classes is casually hung or stored in sight around the room. Sometimes, the work is merely a background, and other times it becomes a focal example of a problem or solution. Students also see each others' work as it is created, hear teachers' comments to peers, and participate directly in commenting on their peers' work in critiques. Student work is ubiquitous in studio classes, and although obvious, its importance in creating an atmosphere of collaboration, peer critique and support, and revision could easily be overlooked and needs to be highlighted.

Professional work is also used as a teaching tool. It models possibilities for artistic problems and solutions, and teachers use it in a wide variety of ways. For example, at Walnut Hill, Jason and Jim set up a show of their own work as the year began. The show introduced the students to their teachers' aesthetic values, attitudes, and skills and sent a clear message to students: Your teachers are working artists.

Such modeling continued throughout the year. Jason brought in collections of pottery made by his potter friends, as well as invitations from their shows, both of which revealed a wide range of variations to consider in the current assignment. Similarly, he set up a computer in a corner of the clay studio and burned CDs that students could borrow, of pictorial sequences of clay-making processes and images of work related to the assignment from other places and eras. Jim brought in stacks of art books and reproductions for his Cubism class, showing individual students examples as they worked on particular problems, and which provided ready material for profitable browsing. He also used works by professional artists to help students visualize problems, as he did by showing pieces by Hopper and Diebenkorn when introducing the assignment to express relationships between figures.

At the Boston Arts Academy, Mickey frequently used art magazines to illustrate design principles and challenges. Beth made copies of images of traditional African vessel types. Kathleen gave a slide show as she introduced the assignment to make self-portraits in hats and vests. In addition, teachers set up contacts with practicing artists and other members of the art world, such as curators, restorers, and designers. Students visited museums and studios, and reported back to the class. And artists visited classes and worked with students—e.g., artists from the Institute of Contemporary Art worked with students at Boston Arts Academy on a sculpture project.

Reflecting on Work at Different Stages of Completion

Artwork, and particularly student artwork, is not just looked at and talked about when it is "done." The teachers we observed held critiques on sketches, on works in midprocess, on completed works, and on bodies of work from a semester, year, or from all 4 years of high school. Critiques at different stages have different functions: Critiques of works in progress can help students hold their initial plans more loosely and consider different ways of completing their work. Critiques of finished works or bodies of work can help students think and talk about what they have accomplished and imagine the next challenges they might face.

Keeping Talk About Artwork Grounded

The teachers we observed worked to keep talk about artworks firmly grounded on specific pieces. As they commented on a piece, they gestured toward aspects of the work that illustrated their words. Jason, for example, often held and encouraged students to touch, rub, hold, and use the ceramic objects in the studio—and also those that students had previously made and taken home already. During critiques, students are encouraged to point out parts of the work that interest them or connect to a point they wish to make. As words are connected to visuals, ideas become more clear and concrete.

Selecting and Arranging Work Intentionally

Teachers select and arrange works to encourage students to draw thoughtful comparisons among them. For example, at the start of the assignment in which students built sculptures from repeating elements ("unit" sculptures), Jason asked students to examine structures that repeated units, such as stacks of plaster molded bottles, a brick wall, and a fired mud-wasp's nest. As conversations about works progress, teachers focus on works that illustrate a point particularly well, often by physically moving a piece to the center of the temporary display. Every work need not be discussed in every critique. Sometimes, the point is to look exhaustively at how each student completed the assign-

ment; at other times, central ideas can be discussed more cogently and vividly by looking at a single work. Of course, it is important for all students to receive regular response to their work, but setting up the expectation that not all pieces will be discussed in *every* conversation is helpful in making looking at artwork a more flexible part of the studio routine.

Using the Work to Illustrate Key Concepts

When teachers give an assignment, not all students may understand key concepts. Looking at artwork allows a chance to revisit and illustrate the central ideas. For instance, Jason describes how examining finished student work helps students realize the importance of attending to small details of ceramic craft.

> Things do become, I think, a lot clearer when the work is finished. . . . I may have been talking about how not to leave a sharp edge on a trimmed foot. And after the pot is fired and it comes out, . . . you can almost cut your hand if they didn't smooth something out. So things like that become amplified. . . . and hopefully [they] recall . . . information that I gave them earlier . . . it was in the back of their mind—but now . . . it solidifies. And their example's right there in front of them.

Now, with these elements of studio classrooms in mind, we turn attention to describing the three Studio Structures—the macrostructures that studio teachers use to organize time, space, and interactions with and among students in efforts to facilitate their learning.

FOUR

Studio Structures

THREE FLEXIBLE TEACHING FORMATS

Over the course of a semester, class time can be organized in many different ways to support (or obstruct) student learning. Different goals and projects require their own instructional shapes. The studio arts teachers we studied organized space, time, and interactions in their classes by using variations on just three Studio Structures: *Demonstration–Lectures*, *Students-at-Work*, and *Critiques*.

The three Studio Structures foster an apprentice–master-craftsman relationship between student and teacher: These structures help create an atmosphere in which student artists work as artists with other artists (teachers and peers). Each structure supports different aspects of student learning. Demonstration–Lectures convey information, so they forecast whatever the assignment is meant to teach (e.g., *Expression* for an assignment focusing on the emotionally evocative space between figures; *Envisioning* for an assignment focused on imagining a vessel that would suit a particular ritual purpose). The Students-at-Work structure emphasizes the growth and development of individual students, because it keeps the *making* of art at the center of the learning experience and allows teachers to shift attention flexibly from student to student and to carefully observe students and evidence of their learning as they work. Thus, we see the Students-at-Work structure as the one that most helps teachers attend to an individual student's "zone of proximal development" (Vygotsky, 1978, 1984)—the range within which an individual can learn when supported by a more competent other. And Critiques support a dynamic flow of thinking among teachers and students that connects the *intended* learning in particular assignments with the ongoing *enacted* learning

of individual students.

In addition to these three *learning* structures, we defined a fourth *management* structure, *Studio Transitions*. Classes always began and ended with Studio Transitions, and sometimes midclass transitions also occurred (e.g., breaks). The teachers found different ways to minimize the time spent in transitions (e.g., set-up and clean-up), which, unless carefully managed, can use up a lot of time that could be spent on learning. For example, since getting started and cleaning up can impinge profoundly on time for learning, the teachers we observed spent a good deal of time in the beginning of the year establishing management routines to keep transitions from unduly interfering with time for art-making. Teachers showed students where and how materials and tools are stored, assigned roles for cleaning up the studio, and created individual spaces for students to store their work and materials.

Teachers varied and sequenced these structures in a host of ways, depending on their goals and projects. The most basic way teachers employed the structures was to begin with a Demonstration–Lecture, followed by a Students-at-Work segment, and concluding with a Critique. Many times, however, these structures were ordered differently, lasted for varying lengths of time, and were repeated within a single class. Teachers also made many modifications within each type of structure; for example, within Critiques, they might use written or oral forms, employ them in midprocess or for synthesizing learning around finished works, or by focusing talk differently (e.g., on "what bugs you," or "what works"). But all the teaching we observed could be categorized into combinations of these structures.

THE DEMONSTRATION–LECTURE

I'll do demonstrations in throwing—I mean, I try to do it pretty quickly. . . . just so they can have a chance to work. Because I mean, that's really why they are there.

—Jason Green

The *Demonstration–Lecture* is a brief, visually rich lecture by the teacher to the class (or to a small group) that conveys information that students will use immediately. Students see authentic art being made, tools being used, or images of work made by others. Demonstration–Lectures, therefore, offer inspiring models. Here are the basic ingredients:

- *Group Focus.* Demonstration–Lectures have a group focus for efficiency. The teacher demonstrates to the whole group, either to give an overview of a project or of several materials, tools, and/or processes students will use that may require further one-on-one or small group follow-up, or to focus on a single, specific technique that can be employed in the assignment.
- *Visual Emphasis.* Information is presented visually so it engages and informs students. Teachers frequently use images and model processes in Demonstration–Lectures.
- *Immediate Relevance.* Demonstration–Lectures relate to work students will be doing soon.
- *Brevity.* Demonstration–Lectures are brief so as to allow enough class time for students to make and reflect on their work.
- *Connection.* Demonstration–Lectures connect ideas. They relate skills, attitudes, and concepts already introduced to those that will be explored and developed in Students-at-Work and Critique structures of current and future classes. Sometimes, teachers use the informal apprentice–master quality of these class segments to build students' appreciation for the ways that they can serve as resources to each other, suggesting that students who have more experience consult with others.

A Contrast to Traditional Lectures

Art students (as well as students of other disciplines) are often visual thinkers. Visual demonstration captures the attention of such students. In addition, it illuminates complex, multistep thinking for all students, that might otherwise be difficult to understand and remember, and it shows students what artistic expertise looks like. The essential difference between Demonstration–Lectures and traditional lectures is the frequent and often extended use that teachers make of visual examples, including objects (e.g., artworks, still-life objects, tools), images (e.g., books, slides, photographs, posters or cards, electronic media), and processes (e.g., modeling step-by-step how to use materials or tools to accomplish particular intentions). In Demonstration–Lectures, teachers rarely talk for long without referring to something that can be seen.

A second way in which the Demonstration–Lecture diverges from traditional lectures is that the information presented is intended to be immediately useful for carrying out class work and homework. This motivates students to pay attention and helps them maintain focus. Because of the emphasis on brevity in Demonstration–Lectures, interaction among students and teachers may be brief, although teachers do interact with students to varying degrees during these class structures. Occasionally, Demonstration–Lectures even become general class discussions.

Finally, through Demonstration–Lectures, teachers present a wide variety of models for ways to meet and solve visual arts challenges. Through modeling, students learn about the relationships among the materials and tools of a medium, what artists have done in the past with these materials and tools, and what the students might do with them. The information presented is not for the purpose of memorization, but for starting students off in working creatively to make art. Generally, teachers show several approaches or images, so that students use examples as inspiration rather than something to copy. Through modeling, teachers exemplify their beliefs about art and working as artists. In addition to the specific processes and multiple examples introduced in Demonstration–Lectures, the structure exposes students regularly to their teacher as an artist, who is thinking and experimenting purposefully, playfully, autonomously, and collaboratively. The teacher models the methods through which art students as well as mature artists develop artistry.

The Role of Demonstration–Lectures

Through Demonstration–Lectures, teachers introduce what they want students to learn in three general ways:

- Setting tasks (assignments)
- Illustrating concepts
- Modeling processes, approaches, and attitudes

The three examples that follow show how three teachers adapt the Demonstration–Lecture structure to their particular needs.

SETTING TASKS:
AFRICAN POTTERY PROJECT (EXAMPLE 4.1)

While introducing ceramics to the 9th grade at Boston Arts Academy, Beth Balliro leads an interactive Demonstration–Lecture to set up a project in which students are to make pottery in pan-African styles using coil-building and surface-patterning (see also Example 12.2). She uses the Demonstration–Lecture to introduce the new project and show how it relates to research on Africa that the students are conducting in their humanities course. Later, Beth demonstrates coil-building as a technique. In the part of the Demonstration–Lecture described here, Beth sets a practical, theoretical, and cultural/ historical background for the work the students are about to undertake.

As is typical in Demonstration–Lectures, Beth addresses the class as a whole about a project they will start on right away. "We're going to start looking at some context, I guess you could say. Some sort of ideas surrounding the artwork we're about to start making." The Demonstration–Lecture is brief, to give students time to explore these ideas in their own artwork. "We're going to fly through this. So don't fall behind. Stay on top of things," Beth tells her students.

Beth starts out by providing some background on African ceramics. She makes it accessible through a story about John Biggers, a contemporary African American artist, and his visual impressions of West African art from a visit to Ghana. Many of her students read below grade level, so Beth structures a shared, oral reading from a short text that students would have had difficulty understanding on their own. The reading is supported by reference to many visual images of ceramic vessels, and these ground the interactive Demonstration–Lecture in the concepts she wants her students to understand (i.e., style, definitions of "art," coil-built pottery, and pattern).

The two-page reading is in a packet dominated by eight pages of images of richly patterned African ceramic vessels made by a coil technique. Through these pictures, Beth engages her students conceptually in identifying and comparing elements of the "style" she wants them to interpret in the creation of their own vessels. "OK, we're going to spend some time during this first part of the class talking, reading, and listening. So get your minds ready to do that. . . . I'm also going to be pointing out a couple of things in your packet." She emphasizes the importance of the concept of *pattern* by pointing to the drawings in the packet and to objects in the room, such as a student's shirt. Then, she asks her students to select three images that would inspire the design of their own vessels. The images allow the students to think about "style" and "pattern," and to envision what they could begin to do with those concepts in their own creations.

Finally, the Demonstration–Lecture serves as the vehicle for connecting the skills and concepts required for this project (coil technique, patterned surfaces on ceramic vessels), the context of African culture (i.e., the focus of their humanities course), and the further skills students will explore later in Students-at-Work and Critique sessions (style, form, other hand-building techniques, and the question of what counts as art within different cultural contexts—a recurring theme in Boston Arts Academy art classes). Thus, the atypical features of this Demonstration–Lecture (e.g., we rarely saw as much interaction or reading as is illustrated here, and we often saw examination of actual objects rather than pictures of objects) illustrate how flexible the structure can be in accommodating the goals of the teacher, the constraints of the context, and the needs of the students.

ILLUSTRATING CONCEPTS:
COIL SCULPTURE PROJECT (EXAMPLE 4.2)

At Walnut Hill, Jason Green uses Demonstration–Lectures extensively to introduce assignments, illustrate concepts, and model use of techniques and tools. In the following example, we see him introducing a project that will involve creating tiles as a way to think about texture on the "skin" of a ceramic sculpture (see also Examples 10.2 and 12.6). Conceptually, Jason wants students to understand the "states of the clay"—that is, states like slip, slurry, plastic, leather-hard, bone-dry, bisque-fired, glaze-fired, and all the intermediate "states" that ceramicists use as their raw material for making art with clay. In addition, he wants students to develop the habits of (1) imagining many possible processes and outcomes and adapting their visions as they work with the material, and (2) pushing themselves to create many possibilities by playing purposefully with the material before they commit to a technique for a finished piece.

The students are in the spring term of their year-long course in ceramics when Jason calls them over to introduce the new assignment:

> The next part of the project after we get your form built, the 3D part built, we're going to put some texture on the outside, . . . So before you do that, you're going to make . . . two flat tiles. One of those tiles is going to use all the states of the clay.

Jason quickly shows the students images of tiles from different cultures and eras, in various styles and shapes, all from photos in a stack of art books he has borrowed from the library. He then demonstrates using a slab roller and a template for sizing the tiles. To help students imagine various possibilities, Jason shows them various processes using hands and hand-tools, including smearing, scratching, cutting against a template, and experimenting with surface textures. As he talks and demonstrates, Jason shows or passes around pieces of clay in different "states": bone-dry, wet or plastic, and slurry. All of this is entirely visual and tactile, whether he's showing the parts of a tool, the steps of a process, or the variation in the material. Jason closes the Demonstration–Lecture with a reminder that he wants students to try things out:

> So it's just going to be experimental. So don't worry too much about it, OK? You want to experiment. You can make a pattern. You might smear this on to the tile [*holding a piece of slurry*]. And find a tool to make a texture in it [*pushing it with his fingernail*]. Or you can then maybe put bone-dry pieces in [*sprinkling some chips of hard clay on the slab*].

Jason demonstrates a lot in a single class, sometimes for over an hour. His demonstrations give students many options and choices about what they might pursue in their own work. Still, considering the scope of the projects and his 3-hour class sessions, Jason's Demonstration–Lectures are comparatively brief, and everything demonstrated is of immediate value in the assigned projects. Finally, everything Jason shows refers back to skills and

concepts he has already introduced and developed; in this case, texturing sculptural surfaces refers back to the surfaces of thrown pots from the first semester. What he demonstrates also foreshadows upcoming concepts and skill—in this case, a tile project that uses molds.

While the five elements of Demonstration–Lecture are clearly evident in Jason's classes, his use of the structure is specific to his goals, to the context of his course and school, and to the needs of the students he is teaching, just as was Beth's very different approach to this structure.

MODELING PROCESSES, APPROACHES, AND ATTITUDES: LIGHT AND BOXES PROJECT   (EXAMPLE 4.3)

About 2 months into his drawing class at Walnut Hill, Jim Woodside introduces an assignment that focuses on light. His Demonstration–Lecture offers students information that will be immediately useful to them and is very short—under 10 minutes for this 3-hour class. Both the brevity and immediacy are prototypical qualities of this structure. Jim's use of Demonstration–Lecture is also prototypical in its use of visual images, emphasis on visual modeling of processes, and in the ways he connects previous work to the new assignment and the new assignment to the future.

Jim uses just a few words to convey the purpose of the assignment to his students ("Light light light light. That's what we're going to work on today."), but he also shows them how it connects to previous work. Students have been drawing all term from observation, and they will do so again today. "All right, what do you notice looking at the still life today?" he asks. This is the same still life that students observed recently when learning perspective drawing—a collection of variously sized and positioned wooden boxes (see also Example 9.2). This week, to emphasize value drawing, the still life is dramatically lit to reveal strong shadows and highlights.

Jim reminds students of previous drawings they have done, suggesting that they use viewfinders as a compositional tool.

> I want you to use the viewfinders like we have in the last couple of weeks—very, very important and helpful in a drawing like this . . . and using an eraser as a tool is not a new idea. Remember how I had said in the past to you:

Using an eraser is not about correcting mistakes, that's what you do with an eraser when you take a math test [*holding up an eraser*]? Using an eraser is just another drawing tool.

In addition, he helps students imagine what finished works might look like by showing drawings that students in other classes have done already for this assignment.

While Jim moves quickly through the purpose of the assignment—naming it explicitly, but not dwelling on it at this early stage in the class because he knows it will make more sense later as students experience challenges and results for themselves; he is careful to model quite deliberately and in some detail how students should approach their own work. He suggests that the project will be easier if they sit on the floor to work, "because a lot of what goes on with drawing this way is going to have to do with gravity." He shows them how to rub charcoal on their paper surfaces to prepare them and how to use a sheet beneath their drawing sheet to catch the extra charcoal that can then be returned to the jar "so we're not wasting it." He also models actually drawing while suggesting ways to begin.

So if I see a white box up there or a strong white tone on the side of one of those shapes [*pointing to the still life*], that's where I'll start. I suggest you start with the lightest forms first, OK [*starting to draw a shape with the eraser; then switching erasers*]? You can get a little bit crisper of an edge with this eraser sometimes. All right?

The materials for the project (i.e., powdered charcoal, kneaded and gum erasers, newsprint) are common and inexpensive. Jim shows students particular characteristics of each material and tool they'll be using.

Each of you is going to have a kneaded eraser [*holding up eraser*]—do all of you know how to work a kneaded eraser? . . . it's self-cleaning, so as it gets black like that—which it will right away—as you use it on this [*pulling at eraser*]—you just sort of pull it and then fold it in on itself, and it'll keep working for a while.

He also wants students to be aware that the charcoal is messy and unhealthy to breathe, so he shows them exactly how to avoid making charcoal dust storms. This is important information for using charcoal and also a way of modeling that artists should be concerned with health and safety issues in the studio.

We want to try to keep this stuff to a minimum in the air, all right? So I don't want to see you like doing this and then blowing it [*pretending to blow on sheet*]—I don't want to have like clouds of this stuff in the air. I mean, it's not going to kill you—it's not—but it's, you know, we just want to try to keep it down so you don't start coughing all day.

In addition, Jim is aware that the technical drawing process of "pulling light out of the piece of paper" may be frustrating for his students. "Obviously this is going to be messy. You're not going to get this sort of nice, pristine perfect drawing, but you're going to learn to see this thing [*pointing to still life*] in terms of shape and light only." He alerts them to common mistakes, such as drawing lines and filling in the shapes, rather than "going right directly to the shape." The drawing tools (erasers) are cruder and more blunt than the tools with which they're most familiar (charcoal, markers, pencils, Craypas, tempera paint), so he also uses the Demonstration–Lecture to make suggestions for how they might work. He suggests they squint as a way to see the simplicity of the shapes.

It gets blurry, and it gets simpler, OK? It's reduced down into real simple forms of light and dark—and that's gonna help you. . . . So here's how we're going to start this. Each of you—to begin with we're going to do an exercise, a small drawing this size on newsprint.

In addition to offering visual information about processes and possibilities, Jim uses the Demonstration–Lecture to set a relaxed, experimental atmosphere about the assignment:

Maybe we will expand to larger drawings today and maybe we'll stick to this size, but let's just start out doing this. . . . We're going to proceed with it and see how it goes. But let's not worry about that just now.

Once again, this structure accommodates the teacher's intentions and purposes for particular students in a particular context.

STUDENTS-AT-WORK

I just call it teaching.

—Kathleen Marsh

The structure we refer to as *Students-at-Work* forms the heart of an art class. Here students work independently on a project, typically one introduced to them in a Demonstration–Lecture. As the students work, the teacher circles the room, offering timely interventions on an informal basis. In a Students-at-Work session, students' primary means for learning about art is through doing. The teacher provides the resources, the challenge, and the individual guidance.

Here are the major characteristics of the Students-at-Work structure:

- *Focus on Making.* Learning occurs mainly through working with materials.
- *Independent Work.* Students work on their own, but in a shared studio space under the guidance of their teacher.
- *Ongoing Assessment.* Teachers observe and assist students while they are working.
- *Individualized Interventions.* Teachers consult with students individually and tailor the assignment and their comments to each student's needs and goals.

Though students usually work individually during these sessions, they do so under the careful guidance of their teacher and in the community of the studio classroom where their classmates are also working. The Students-at-Work structure allows for both independent work and for a collaborative and informal sharing of information, thinking processes, and understanding.

Personalized Teaching

Students-at-Work sessions offer time for teachers to shift from standing at the center of students' attention to observing students as they work. During these sessions, teachers generally work with individual students, personalizing their comments and suggestions. Teachers watch students' work in progress carefully and consult with students one-on-one. These consults may be quick or extended interactions. Consults promote thoughtful decisions. They might include encouraging remarks, brief demonstrations with the materials, questions that help students reflect on their work in progress, or extended conversations about a student's intentions for a piece or about how a particular piece relates to broader goals in the course and to the student's potential for developing as an artist.

The Role of Students-at-Work

Students-at-Work is the cornerstone of the studio classroom. In the 38 class sessions we observed, the largest percentage of time (typically 60–75%) was spent with students working independently on projects while the teacher observed and consulted with students individually about their work.

In the Students-at-Work sessions during class, students are deeply involved with the materials of the assigned project—drawing, painting, sketching, centering pots, or forming objects out of clay; thinking seriously; and making artistic decisions as they work. Students carefully observe their works, plan the next steps of their projects by envisioning changes, and experiment with new techniques, materials, and ideas. Students learn to reflect continually on the processes of using and making decisions about materials.

The teacher plays a key diagnostic role, observing the students working and consulting one-on-one to guide them in their work. The Students-at-Work session has three broad roles in the studio classroom.

- Putting *making* at the center of learning (with perception and reflection growing out of making)
- Assessing work *processes* (not just resulting products)
- *Individualizing* the curriculum

Putting Making at the Center of Learning. Teachers' decisions to devote most of their classroom time to having students make art is what makes an art class a studio class. Students-at-Work sessions give students the time, space, materials, and support they need to create artworks and put into action the ideas that are introduced and discussed during Demonstration–Lectures and Critiques.

Assessing Work Processes. In Students-at-Work sessions, teachers continually assess students in all phases of their working *process*, rather than just evaluating their final *products*. They see students' plans for a piece develop, watch how students start, make decisions, and change directions, and see immediately how students respond to instruction. This observation of students as they work is the fundamental way teachers assess how students' minds are developing as they work and learn. Such immediate observation and response also allows teachers to help students in the moment, often the most effective way to instruct. Students told us that they learned more from their teacher's comments on works in process than comments on their completed works.

Individualizing the Curriculum. In a sense, teachers have two sets of curricula in a studio classroom: one for the whole class, and one for each individual student. This personalized curriculum is developed in response to the specific abilities, needs, and interests of each student. While individualizing is in no way unique to studio art teaching (excellent teachers of all subjects know how to individualize to great advantage), the studio classroom has long used individualization and can provide a model of individualized teaching for the rest of the academic curriculum. As Jim explains, "I do have goals for individual kids . . . each kid is very different. . . . [My studio class] is absolutely equally a class activity and an individual activity." By allowing teachers to gather information about how individual students work and learn, the Students-at-Work sessions enable teachers to define and carry through individualized responses to help particular students along their personal paths of development. Thus, the Students-at-Work structure supports teachers working effectively with heterogeneous skill levels in one classroom.

THE CRITIQUE

That's why we have these critiques. . . . I try to get them to realize that they need to start looking at their results very carefully. . . . I want them to start looking and getting information and applying that back to what they're going to do next.

—Jason Green

Critiques are central to a studio class—a chance for students and teachers to reflect as a group on their work and working process. In Critiques, art-making is paused, so that students and teacher can reflect on the work and the process of creation. Here are four ingredients of Critiques:

- *Focus on Artworks.* The class as a group focuses their attention on their own and other students' work.
- *Reflective.* Students think about the meanings and expressions conveyed by works of art, and think about what is successful, what is not, and why.
- *Verbal.* Students must put their reflections into words as they are asked to describe their working process and products, and to explain and evaluate their artworks.
- *Forward-looking.* The discussion aims to guide individual students' future work and help them envision new possibilities.

Features of Critiques

Critiques do not have a rigid format or single purpose. They are structured in a wide variety of ways, they occur at many different points in the working process, and they are used to further different ends. However, Critiques have two distinguishing features that earn them a place of honor in the studio classroom: First, they focus attention on students' work and working processes. And second, Critiques are explicitly social. Students share their work with the teacher and other students and get responses from them. Taken together, these two features make Critiques an important forum for helping students develop an understanding of their work and development as artists.

The Work Does the Teaching. By focusing on student work, critiques become a powerful teaching tool. Just looking collectively at a piece of art is useful for both students and teachers. When students see the range of ways their classmates have approached an assignment, they begin to envision possibilities outside their usual habits. A concept that eludes a student may suddenly "click" once seen and discussed in a classmate's work. Critiques are where students most genuinely learn from one another.

Teachers, too, find it informative to put up all the work for a Critique. Doing so gives teachers a quick and powerful way to gauge where students are as a group, to see how individuals vary in relation to the group and to expert norms, and how the teacher can best help individuals and the group address their current needs in the next project.

A Community of Arts Learners. Students learn in conversation with others. While students often talk about their own work during Critiques, and teachers also generally comment on individual students' work, Critiques involve an explicit shift from individual to group work as the class comes together as a community to discuss one another's works. Critiques involve sharing work and responses with others. Students gain insight about their own art-making by verbalizing thoughts about their own work, and by hearing how others talk about their work. They also learn by looking at others' works and hearing how these works are discussed. A 9th-grade student in Mickey's design class at the Boston Arts Academy talked about the value of learning from others during critiques:

> After we did art pieces, we'd sit down together and talk about it. And that helps a lot because you get . . . certain opinions or advice from not just the teacher but the students around you better observing your work. And you could take that advice and use it on the next piece.

The Role of Critiques

In Critiques, students and teachers look back on art that is being or has recently been made by the students. The purpose is to understand and evaluate students' work and working process, and to look forward as individual students begin to envision possibilities for how to proceed. Critiques can take many forms, and teachers structure them to suit particular students' needs and to address goals for the class as a whole. In the 38 classes we observed, there were 25 Critiques, ranging from a 2.5-minute session to a 2.5-hour-long session with seniors who had been working independently for the previous month. Critiques offer a forum for balancing the learning opportunities of an assignment with the particular needs and insights of individual students in a dynamic interplay.

Each of the teachers we observed structured Critiques differently. But for all teachers, Critiques played the following key roles in fostering learning in the arts:

Helping Students Connect Their Working Process to the Final Product. In the Critiques we observed, students' artworks are not viewed as static objects to be evaluated, but rather as a record of the students' thinking and making process. A key aim

of the Critique is to make explicit and analyze the decisions that went into making a piece.

Critiques often employ a reverse engineering technique in which students and teachers try to understand how something was made; identify the effects of different decisions, marks, and techniques; and imagine how the work could have been made differently. For instance, as Jason's students pick up and examine ceramic pieces, he asks them to notice evidence of the artists' hands on the pieces and think about how the pieces appear to have been made, why they were made that way, and what they would look like had the artist made them differently.

The product is not the only thing that matters in assessment—students are praised for stretching beyond their usual style or habits of working, even if the resulting artwork is not particularly successful. Conversely, a successful piece may be criticized if the student did not venture outside his or her "comfort zone" to make it. Works are often praised in terms of the thought process behind them: "a smart solution," "a really powerful decision."

Helping Students Learn to Observe, Interpret, Explain, and Evaluate Works. Artworks can seem impenetrable to students. While students can often tell whether or not they like a piece, they have to learn to understand and notice how different aspects of a work contribute to its general effect. Through Critiques, teachers instruct students in how to notice details and patterns in artworks, how to understand what the works communicate and why, how to verbalize what they see, and how to evaluate the effectiveness of works. A key aim of Critiques is to help students explain what they see, think, and feel about work and working.

Teachers push students to notice more dimensions of the work by asking them to focus on particular aspects rather than just the whole. For instance, Kathleen asks her students to talk about the composition for each self-portrait, and Mickey asks students to think about how light acts as a subject in each of their photographs. This narrower focus helps students organize their thinking about artworks and pushes them to think beyond the novice response of "I like it."

Teachers model how they want students to look at and think about artworks. They often talk aloud through their thought process as they view a work. They point out details and features that they notice, they describe what the work reminds them of or the feelings it evokes, and they articulate visions of how the piece would look if a part were changed. The aim is not to communicate an authoritative interpretation of a work, but rather to model a process of thinking about it (*Reflect*).

Teachers may give general strategies for thinking about and evaluating work. For instance, Jim tells his senior Critique group to ask themselves the question, "What part of a work seems most extraneous? What could be taken away, and the central thrust of the work would remain the same?" He tells them this strategy can be a useful way to push work forward when there's nothing obviously wrong with it—a way to improve a piece that is already successful.

Highlighting Key Concepts in the Assignment or Course. While the assignments in the classes we observed were open-ended and not prescriptive, they often served as a targeted exploration of an artistic concept or concepts such as value, expression, line, sculptural unit, or abstraction. At the Boston Arts Academy, these key concepts were often formalized in an assignment rubric. At Walnut Hill, they tended to be more informally presented in the teacher's instructions, description, or demonstration of the assignment. Teachers often used Critiques to highlight these concepts in students' work.

In addition, each teacher had a number of key ideas that he or she touched upon over and over throughout the year. For instance, Jim repeatedly stressed the idea that technique should serve expressive purposes and that expressive, emotional aspects of works arise from the ordinary. On the very first day of class, he helped students see the expressive potential of a still life of a collection of objects painted white, and, in Critiques throughout the year, he repeatedly revisited the relationship between technique and expression. Teachers have a variety of key ideas, such as examining the relationships between form and function, observation and abstraction, or that between the students' artwork and their lives. During Critiques, teachers point to ways in which students' work illustrates aspects of these central ideas, and suggest ways students could incorporate or develop them in their work.

Guiding Students' Future Work. Critiques look back at what has been done to help shape students' work on the current piece-in-progress and on the pieces they will make in the future. Sometimes this guidance is explicit: Students receive specific suggestions, whether for the piece being critiqued or for the next assignment. The guidance may also be implicit: Teachers instill the idea that each project should be reflected on and should inform future work, as Jason said in the lead quotation for this section. Critiques encourage students to push beyond just looking at the work "as is" and help them develop the habit of envisioning new possibilities for what it could become.

Critiques extend beyond reflections on the work itself, because fundamentally they are reflections by students about themselves as developing artists. Teachers help students see elements that are characteristic of their work, and help them identify strengths on which to build. Teachers learn about their students' approaches to work not only by observing the works but also by listening to what their students *say*. For instance, after a Critique, Jim noted about one student: "I think that she's really finding a way to draw here. Now I know that I know this from talking to her a lot and looking at her other drawings. But she's finding a way to draw that is really smart and really her own." Through Critiques, students develop an understanding of their personal way of working and the ways that this personal style may differ from that of other students in the class.

VARIATIONS IN THE USE OF THE STUDIO STRUCTURES

Teachers weave the three Studio Structures of Demonstration–Lecture, Students-at-Work, and Critiques together in many different ways, but the classes we observed usually fell into one of two basic shapes.

ABA Shape

In a classic art-school model of a studio class, students work in long stretches of unbroken time, sandwiched within an introduction and conclusion. We refer to this pattern of whole-group–individual–whole-group structures as the ABA shape (see Figure 4.1). We saw teachers employ it frequently.

The class begins with a whole group gathering, such as in a Demonstration–Lecture in which an assignment or working process is explained. Or, the class might begin with a brief Critique of work from a previous class that leads into work for the current class. That's the "A" section of the ABA shape. The class then shifts to an individualized Students-at-Work session for the bulk of the class period (60–75%

of the class time)—the "B" of the shape. The class concludes by returning to whole-group time, with either a Critique of the work made during the class, or a Demonstration–Lecture reviewing what was learned and highlighting what will come in the next class—this is the closing "A" of the ABA shape.

Figure 4.1. Time Bar Showing the ABA Class Shape
From Kathleen Marsh's class, session 8, Mounting the Show Project

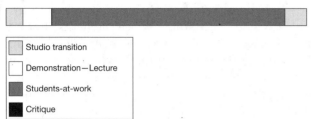

Sometimes teachers would spread this ABA shape over two classes. For instance, at the Boston Arts Academy, Mickey, who had shorter class sessions than some of the other teachers (1.5 hours twice a week compared with 3 hours once a week), sometimes spent one class introducing and getting students started on a project (Demonstration–Lecture followed by Students-at-Work), and then used the next session as an entirely unbroken work session followed only by clean-up (Students-at-Work followed by studio transition). This allowed students to enter into their work deeply (*Engage and Persist*) and lessened the amount of time spent setting up and cleaning up materials.

Punctuated Shape

The second approach we observed to shaping class time employs shorter structures layered more frequently and at shorter intervals within a single class. We call this type of sequence a punctuated shape (see Figure 4.2). This, too, was used commonly to organize class time.

The class might begin with a quick Critique of work from the previous class, followed by a short Demonstration–Lecture to introduce the current assignment. Then students might move into a brief Students-at-Work session, followed by a second Critique to reflect on their work in progress. They

might then return to Students-at-Work, followed again by Critique, then by a third Students-at-Work session, before a final Demonstration–Lecture extends the assignment with a new twist and ends the class.

Figure 4.2. Time Bar Showing the Punctuated Class Shape
From Jim Woodside's class, session 1, working on the Contour Drawing Project

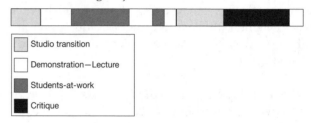

Such interspersion gives teachers more opportunities to refocus students on the habits that teachers intend them to learn, to help the group build thinking together about their work (*Reflect*), and to introduce new ideas incrementally, rather than with heavy doses of Demonstration–Lecture as class begins, which requires students to sustain focus independently.

We cannot claim to know which forms are best, nor even whether any one form *is* best, nor can we recommend how much of each type is sufficient, nor suggest best practices for selecting how to mix ABA and punctuated classes to result in maximal learning. We do have hypotheses: Punctuated classes seem to be more effective with younger, less skilled or invested students, or when projects have multiple technical steps. ABA classes may be most effective with older or more skilled students, or at stages in a project in which students are already deeply engaged. But at this stage of the framework's development, we can only identify and describe the structures, habits, and shapes we observed. We suspect that there is no "most effective" way, but, rather, many ways that serve different goals and populations. As teachers work with the structures over time, preferences and best practices will certainly emerge; future research can then compare various approaches for efficacy in promoting learning.

STUDIO HABITS OF MIND: *WHAT* THE ARTS TEACH

Watch an entire studio art class with the aim of discovering what kind of thinking is being taught in this class, and you will see that what is going on is a lot more complex than the teaching of craft. Of course, students are learning technique—they learn to throw a pot on the wheel, they learn to mix colors, they learn to draw in proportion using perspective. But they learn so much more.

Whenever students were learning craft, they were also being taught a variety of other kinds of important skills and attitudes. We counted eight (including craft) which we call the *Studio Habits of Mind*. In the chapters that follow in Part II we describe each one of these in alphabetical order:

Develop Craft   *Observe*
Engage and Persist   *Reflect*
Envision   *Stretch and Explore*
Express   *Understand the Art World*

These habits of mind are undeniably important—learning to see, learning to persist, learning to judge, and more. Only further research will tell us whether these habits are the same or different when learned in a studio arts class or in academic classes. And only further research will tell us whether these learning habits transfer to other areas of the curriculum. Might students who develop the habit of Persisting from weeks learning to throw six-inch clay cylinders bring this newly developed habit into crafting and drafting essays? Might students who hone their observational skills in a studio art class apply this habit to their work with microscopes in biology class? We don't know the answers to these kinds of questions about "transfer" of learning to non-arts classrooms, but we do know that before we can talk about transfer, we first need to figure out what is learned in the primary domain of art.

FIVE

Learning to Develop Craft

USING ART TOOLS, MATERIALS, AND CONCEPTS

You start and you don't know how to do anything. You make a huge mess. You're out of control. You have no technique. It's so obvious [laughing], 'cause it's so messy. And then like any craft, you have to build and build and practice and practice. And the minute you create something with control and with technique—it's just a totally beautiful moment because you know you couldn't do it before.

—Beth Balliro

They know when they need to be there. They . . . just work . . . they've just developed studio habits. . . . And they work like artists. They just come in and do their work, and they know where everything goes. . . . And that's what you want the beginning students to develop into.

—Jason Green

Perhaps the most obvious *Studio Habit of Mind* that students learn in an art class is to learn technique, or craft. Students acquire the dispositions to work with purposeful attention in various media, and we refer to this as *Develop Craft: Technique*. Students also learn to care for materials and tools, and we refer to this as *Develop Craft: Studio Practice*. When we analyzed our videotapes and interviews, we labeled as Technique all instances when students were being taught how to *use* tools, materials, and procedures; we labeled as Studio Practice all instances when students were being taught how to *take care of* tools and materials. We then combined these two broad dispositions into a single Studio Habit of Mind that we call Develop Craft, described in this chapter.

TEACHING STUDENTS TO UNDERSTAND TECHNIQUE

As students develop technique, they learn to use a variety of tools (e.g., viewfinders, brushes, pottery wheels) and materials (e.g., charcoal, paint, clay). Teachers demonstrate the use of tools and materials and guide students as they work. Students are meant to learn the varied properties of tools and materials and the range of ways that they can be employed in a skilled and mindful way. Students develop a sense of what they can and cannot do with different tools and materials, and they become more adept at choosing the right tools and materials for the piece they wish to make.

As students develop technique, they also learn about the elements of artworks, such as form, line, surface, value, and how to employ artistic conventions such as perspective or color mixing. While developing technique involves becoming familiar with artistic conventions, it does not require rigid adherence to them. Developing technique allows students to make informed decisions about if and when to depart from conventions or use tools and materials in new ways.

Developing technique was emphasized as an intended learning in every studio class we observed. But we almost never saw technique taught as an isolated skill. Tools, materials, conventions, and skills were introduced in the context of larger projects that required students to "think with these skills," rather than as tricks to be mastered for their own sakes.

Students told us about how hard they worked on their technique, and in their comments showed how learning technique was inextricably related to learning other Studio Habits of Mind. For instance, a senior from the Boston Arts Academy talked about working on capturing light and creating variations of value in his drawing, and his comments show us how this work relates his learning of Develop Craft to Engage and Persist and to *Observe*.

> It's about capturing light on something. . . . Once more it's about value. Because that's something I've been working on the past four years. . . . I push myself to see more variations and to get more detailed and to compare the grays. Like when I was doing my self-portrait, comparing the grays between one area of my face and the other to try to show the difference [see Figure 5.1].

Figure 5.1. Self-Portrait from a Senior at the Boston Arts Academy

TEACHING THE THEORY AND PRACTICE OF COLOR: INVENTING COLORS PROJECT   (EXAMPLE 5.1)

The classroom example that follows illustrates *Developing Craft: Technique*. In a color-mixing class at the Boston Arts Academy, Beth Balliro teaches her students about color theory and how to use the color wheel. They put this into practice by experimenting with color mixing using acrylic paints.

Beth's Inventing Colors Project (see also Examples 7.1 and 13.1), taught near the midpoint of her second-semester course with 9th-graders, is part of her multiweek Imaginary Creatures Painting Project in which students depict themselves as a mythical creature. Two paintings are assigned in this class. In the first, students depict where their creature was born, focusing on using a set of complementary colors. In the second, they depict where their creature died, focusing on using a set of neutral colors. The class is intended to help students gain experience with acrylic paints before they begin using them on their final paintings, where they will put into practice some of what they have learned about color theory.

Demonstration–Lecture

Beth begins her Inventing Colors session with a Demonstration–Lecture on color theory that focuses on the color wheel. Beth tells students that color theory is a topic that can be taught at many levels and requires gradual building up of knowledge.

> You're getting the basics of color theory. . . . This is a very, very first baby step. And when you're sophomores and make it back here, you'll need to know this. When you're juniors you'll further refine it. And, when you're seniors, you'll laugh because this will be so easy. OK, but right now it's the first, first step. It's the foundation. And, unless you know the foundation, you can't build upon it.

Beth directs students' attention to a color wheel she has drawn on the board. Using the wheel, she engages students in a question-and-answer session about various aspects of color theory: primary and secondary colors, complementary colors, neutral colors, and color mixing. She builds on students' knowledge, elicits and corrects misconceptions, and models how to use the wheel to envision new colors. She also explains that the color wheel is a theoretical construct that provides guidelines for color mixing, but that learning about color also involves trial-and-error mixing with the specific paint being used.

Studio Transition

While students distribute the brushes, papers, and palettes (i.e., clean, white Frisbees), Beth reminds them about how they need to care for materials (Develop Craft: Studio Practice) and shows them how to set up their palettes with only red, blue, yellow, white, and a gloss medium. She directs students' attention to writing on the board that describes the guidelines for the two assigned paintings. As students are setting up their palettes and materials, Beth checks in with individuals to make sure they understand the assignment.

Students-at-Work

As students work with the paint, Beth encourages them to experiment and mix a wide range of colors in order to build an understanding of the concepts of complementary and neutral colors.

- *Invent your own colors and use principles of color theory to move beyond basic colors.* Beth tells one student,

> Yellow/violet. Those are opposites, so have it be mostly yellow and then mostly violet. So yellow doesn't mean only this [*holding up a yellow paint tube*]. You can mix it with a little red to have an orangish yellow, or a little white to have a whitish yellow.

Stopping to talk with another student, she reminds him to use the painting to develop facility with color mixing and not to spend too much time locked into detail. Moving to two other students, Beth advises one to explore "endless kinds of yellow." With the second, she clarifies, "You don't want it to be just red or green, you want it to be in the family of red or green."

- *Use principles of color theory to guide your color mixing.* To a student who asks how to achieve skin tone by mixing colors, Beth demonstrates as she tells him how to make use of the principles of color theory along with trial and error to create a desired color: "Whenever you go for skin, that's a neutral color no matter whose skin you're talking about. And that's made by mixing the color and its opposite." She also points out that she's using lots of water because she wants the colors to blend. Finally she shows how to add white for a highlight, but cautions:

> If you want to get darker, you can't use black because it will make it too gray—I want you to do what a group of artists

called the Impressionists did, which is to use only color for dark. So I'm going to add [*adding blue*] and this will be your dark.

- *Think of these paintings as a vehicle to develop technique in color mixing.* Beth tells one student:

> Try not to spend too much time on the drawing. Because even though we just spent lots of time talking about how drawing is the foundation of painting, today you need to learn how to mix color. That's the goal of today. It's not to create a great perspective drawing of a bridge. It's to mix color.

- *Recognize that trial and error help in learning to mix color.* Beth asks a student what he used to mix the color he wants to be a deep orange. As she demonstrates how to mix the color, Beth explains, "So if I said that orange is a little too green, add red, the opposite of green. It's a back and forth. There is no recipe because each kind of paint acts differently."
- *Try other ways to mix color once you have grasped basic techniques.* Beth confirms a student's use of red plus yellow to make orange, with the addition of gel medium to make a translucent orange. Then she challenges him:

> And now think about if you can pull in other colors to get it to be even more of a range of color. In other words, now that I've seen a lot of paintings I think, "Oh he made that with red and yellow." You want me to look at it and not even care about how you made it. You want me to think, "Ah, look at that red. How did he do that? It's a mystery red."

Beth Reflects

Beth explained to us in a post-class interview that she lectures on the color wheel and its history rather than just letting students learn through trial and error so that students will see that painting is scientific. Regardless of whether or not students become painters, "they understand that painting is not exclusively an intuitive, free, emotional process, but there is a real science supporting it, and a long history of color theory."

But theory is not enough. To explain why students also need to experiment with paint, Beth gave the following example of what colors do in practice to model differences from what the color wheel predicts:

> If you mix Yellow Ochre with Mars Black you get a green. So without any kind of blue, you can achieve a green. And that's very different from what the color wheel tells you. And it's because how they make Mars Black is with probably some dark, dark blue pigment. It's a composite color so it's not a pure thing.

In her Demonstration–Lecture, she alerts students to this gap between theory and practice. This class illustrates Beth's belief that playful assignments that prompt students to *Stretch and Explore* help students develop technique. She explained that when students play around, they end up having to confront technical issues. And when students are just playing around, Beth finds she can help them with technical issues in a low-stakes way without threatening their self-confidence.

With more advanced students, Beth uses a more complex and inventive approach to technique instead of explicitly focusing on the development of technical skills, as she does with beginners. "I believe in the standard 'you have to know the rules to break them,' and this connects to building technique first and then pushing beyond it and its foundation," she explains. For beginners, Beth said she might ask them to use five complementary colors, while with advanced painters she might talk about achieving space through the sharpness of edges, or by *inventing* some kind of technique. Beth also added another example: "With 9th-graders I might talk about . . . how you glaze. This is how you create a dry brush effect. With an upper-grade student, I might say 'what technique have you made up here?'"

TEACHING STUDENTS TO UNDERSTAND STUDIO PRACTICE

Studio art involves making things, and students need facility with the tools and materials with which these things are made. Some instruction must invariably involve teaching students conventions for caring for materials and tools. We call this kind of instruction *Develop Craft: Studio Practice*. Studio Practice refers to ways for finding, caring for, and storing materials (e.g., clay, paper, paint) and tools (e.g., brushes, wire cutters, erasers). Studio Practice also involves learning how to store one's works—labeling and dating

them, spraying them, putting them in portfolios so they do not get ripped, and so forth. This is distinguished from learning how to present one's work with matting and framing, which we classified as Understand Art World: Domain, because it involves learning to present oneself as an artist. Studio Practice also involves learning ways to make best use of the physical space of the classroom (e.g., giving yourself ample room for materials, placing materials such that they are easy to use where and when you need them), as well as learning about procedures that are specific to work in an art studio (e.g., wearing smocks, wearing safety glasses when using power tools).

The two classroom examples that follow illustrate Developing Craft: Studio Practice.

TEACHING THE PRACTICE OF MAINTAINING THE STUDIO: SELF-PORTRAITS IN COLORED PENCIL PROJECT   (EXAMPLE 5.2)

At the Boston Arts Academy in Kathleen Marsh's class, Self-Portraits in Colored Pencil, taught near the beginning of her fall course with 9th-graders (see also Example 10.3), students engage in a clean-up session that shows many of the features of what we came to call Studio Practice. From the first days of school, Kathleen assigns specific clean-up tasks to students in her 9th-grade class as a way of encouraging them to be responsible for maintaining their work environment. Kathleen considers it foundational that students learn the studio practices of setting up, cleaning up, coming in and out of the studio space, and finding specific tools and materials. She notes, "It's going to be a huge change from what they've been doing." Workspaces inevitably get messy, and students must learn that cleaning up is just as important as setting up their work environment.

In interviews with us, Kathleen stressed the importance of students learning to maintain their work environment, which is especially important in a shared space. If students have their own studio, the level of mess is a personal choice. But in a communal space, courtesy and efficiency dictate cleaning up. "There are so many people that use that room. That room is in use all day long. And it's got to be ready and presentable for the next class." She used the example of Alexander Calder to acknowledge how working solo differs. "I don't think the man ever cleaned up. And it didn't affect his work any. Some people have to have a clean environment to work. But I don't think everybody does." In a shared space, Kathleen added, "It's about citizenship."

Kathleen teaches clean-up as part of a work cycle. "They have to understand that their work period has a beginning and an end, and at the end, you know, the work has to go in a place where you're going to be able to find it. And the tables have to be orderly. And the floor has to be swept. That's just basic." To structure the clean-up, Kathleen assigns specific tasks so students know exactly for which part they are responsible. Assignments provide training and solve the practical problem of making sure all work gets done. Kathleen also told us that at the Boston Arts Academy there is a school-wide clean-up philosophy. "This is their workspace, so they need to work on maintaining it."

Teaching the Studio Practice of Keeping a Portfolio: Light and Boxes Project   (Example 5.3)

Midway through the first term, students in Jim Woodside's class are working on a Light and Boxes Project (see also Examples 4.3 and 9.2). They are making reverse charcoal drawings of a still life of boxes by using an eraser to pull light forms out of paper coated with graphite. Today students are also going to learn how to care for their work by constructing a portfolio, spraying their drawings so that they don't get smudged, and organizing and storing their artworks in the portfolio. During class, Jim takes students one at a time over to the side of the room, where he helps them make a portfolio from cardboard and duct tape.

Before students start to draw, Jim explains what they will be doing and why. "I think the easiest way, the most useful way to maximize our time is for me to ask you to come over one-by-one. And then the rest of you can keep drawing." He also reminds students to spray their drawings outside where there's fresh air, to preserve them. Jim makes clear to students that portfolios help them take care of their work. Additionally, he tells them that having work organized in portfolios helps him when he grades their work.

Jim Reflects

In an interview, Jim talked about the importance of students keeping portfolios of their work. Maintaining a portfolio helps instill a sense of professionalism in students about their artwork, an important sense that takes time for students to learn. Portfolios also allow students to see changes from their early to later drafts. Seeing this history of one's working

process is part of seeing oneself as an artist, and this is the reason Jim encourages students not to throw away any of their work.

It's really important, because it has to do with how they see themselves as artists. They see the work they've produced. They see the process they've been in. And they see the history of the process. This is why I don't want them to throw things away as well. You know, sometimes I say, "If you do something that you think is a mistake and you throw it away, it doesn't mean you never made the mistake, you know. So why throw it away?"

When Jim sits down to write comments and give grades, he looks through a portfolio to view a student's work from the beginning to the end of the semester. Students looking at their portfolios have the same window onto their work and working process. They see the peaks and valleys and how hard they've worked, and this allows them to reflect on their process and progress. Additionally, Jim told us that he worked one-on-one because students in this class were young, and he wanted to sit with each of them personally as they organized their work. Here is why he had students cut the portfolios out of cardboard:

I think it's good wherever I can to teach kids to take shortcuts about art supplies, because so many art supplies are so expensive. And the kids need to learn to be resourceful and make things—even the kids that do have money. I just think basic to being an artist is a kind of resourcefulness.

STRUCTURING A CLASS TO FOCUS ON BOTH TECHNIQUE AND STUDIO PRACTICE

Teaching Care of the Wheel and Throwing Technique: Introducing Centering on the Wheel   (Example 5.4)

At Walnut Hill, Jason Green develops students' understanding of Studio Practice and Technique in his Centering Project, introduced in the first class of the fall semester (see also Example 14.1). Here students begin to learn how to use the pottery wheel to center balls of clay. To do this, they must gain familiarity with both rules of the studio and techniques for using the pottery wheel (see Figure 5.2).

Figure 5.2. Develop Craft—Jason Green's Students Learn to Throw Clay Forms on a Pottery Wheel

A. Jason Green introduces tools to students in their first ceramics class

B. Jason labels drawers of ceramics tools to make them accessible

C. Jason demonstrates setting up to center clay on a pottery wheel

D. Jason works with students individually on centering

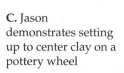

Demonstration–Lecture

At the beginning of this first class, Jason shows students where the tools and materials they will need are kept. In this 15-minute Demonstration–Lecture, he walks them through setting up materials and tools so they can begin to work. As he talks, he demonstrates each tool, shows how it works, and then gives step-by-step instructions as he shows how to work the wheel, showing both correct and incorrect ways.

The following examples show how Jason introduces getting set up to use the pottery wheel:

- *Jason tells students all about the tools they will need (Develop Craft: Studio Practice).* Jason informs students that they will each need a bucket for water. He shows them where the buckets are kept and fills one with water to show exactly where and how to fill them, as well as how much water to put in. He also shows students ceramics tools that they will need. He takes one of each and displays the collection on a nearby table as an example that they can refer to as they set up their own throwing materials—wooden ribs, wire tools, needle tools, and sponges—and other tools that they won't need today but will use later, like wooden knives.
- *Jason tells students how to get their clay ready for the wheel (Develop Craft: Technique).* Students will first need to get water in a bucket and set up a bat, the round flat surface on which their clay will sit as they turn the wheel and work the clay. Jason shows students how to cut clay and how to compress it. As he demonstrates, Jason describes what he's doing. "When I'm doing this, I'm trying not to fold the clay, like these folds, really trying to keep those compressed."
- *Jason gives a detailed description of the wheels (Develop Craft: Studio Practice).* Jason holds up a splash pan, shows how this large bowl fits onto the wheels, and notes that some of the wheels are a little bit different; these practical details are critical to the students' success with the tools. He next shows how each wheel has a pedal and where the buttons are that turn the wheels on. Students will also need a bat. Jason tells students where to get their bats and how to care for them.

> Sometimes the bats aren't cleaned. You want to make sure everything's clean. So if you have clay here [*pointing to the bat*],

or clay around these [*pointing to the wheel surface where there are pins that fit the holes in the bat*], you might need to take your needle tool and clean it a little bit [*holds up the needle tool*].

Once a bat is clean, it can be placed on bat pins, and students are told to be sure that the bat doesn't rock on its pins.

Next, Jason shows students how to form balls of clay. He makes eight balls to give students a chance to really see his ball-making technique as they work along. After they have made several balls themselves, Jason demonstrates how to center a ball of clay on the wheel. As he demonstrates, Jason carefully describes all the actions involved in each step of the process. He draws their attention to how his body is positioned, where his support is, and what he does with his hands. As he demonstrates the correct procedures, he also describes typical problems students may have and how to avoid them.

Students-at-Work

Following Jason's introduction, students choose a wheel and set up their own areas for work. Jason talks with students as they work, offering comments rich in information about the studio practice of getting set up. Sometimes Jason's comments remind students of what they saw in the earlier Demonstration–Lecture, as when he had to remind students where to get their clay. Other comments offer new information, as when he told students which kind of bat to use.

When students begin to work on the wheel, Jason circles the room, closely observing students before giving advice on their technique. When he talks with students, he notes points of success and corrects errors, frequently demonstrating again as he talks. The repetition is necessary to support understanding, as each student sees new aspects of the process, depending on their constantly changing levels of understanding.

- *Jason reminds students of the assignment and gives advice as he watches them (Develop Craft: Technique).* When students first start working, Jason often reminds them of the assignment and what he has shown them in the Demonstration–Lecture. For example, stopping to look at the balls of clay one student has made, he reminds her,

Make these really, really round. Make eight and remember you'll need a bat, which is up front, to put them on. Try to make them the same size if you can. That's good, that's good. Try not to make them too big; you'll have to use lots of muscle.

- *Jason gives step-by-step instructions to help students attend to aspects of process as they work (Develop Craft: Technique).* To a student trying the complex process of starting the wheel and centering a clay ball, Jason first advises, "Now, the first thing, you're going to put some water on it and press down on it." He then corrects how fast she is spinning the wheel. After the student has correctly adjusted the speed, Jason demonstrates and describes how to hold her hands and press the clay. Before moving to the next student Jason prompts, "Add a little bit more water now," and demonstrates again how the student should hold her hands.
- *Jason shows how the whole body contributes to centering (Develop Craft: Technique).* As Jason advises students, he moves students' hands, elbows, or feet to correct their position or demonstrates proper form himself. Jason tells one student, "Remember, your left elbow has to be braced, so you want to brace it against your hip. And then you want to put your right hand, lock it onto your left hand." As he speaks, he shows her this technique and how the clay is starting to get centered as he starts to apply pressure. After watching the student, he reminds her, "Keep that elbow down on your leg. Put pressure on the top and side at the same time, and add water very frequently."

Jason Reflects

In an interview after the class, Jason told us that he focuses on the technique of centering because that skill is a prerequisite to making any kind of pottery. He added that in the demonstration he shows how to center rather than how to make a pot because "students know they're going to be making pottery, and they know pottery is hollow. But if they don't have that basic skill of centering, then it's very, very difficult to make a pot."

Jason explained that centering is a complex and difficult skill that involves a variety of types of understanding—conceptual and physical—and that his goal in the first several weeks is for students to learn to center.

Most of them have never touched clay before. And even if you know a little bit about throwing pottery, you know what centering is, but if it's brand new, you might not even know what that term means. In some ways there are mechanical and sensory aspects and the understanding that goes along with it—understanding the language of the medium.

Jason's focus on centering is one way he works to change students' general attitudes toward materials. Jason gave us the following reason for his emphasis on the properties of clay:

Sometimes students will try to use clay to make something, and they're just making their idea and not *thinking* about the material. And they may fail, because they're not using the entire process. They're just using the clay as a construction material.

Without becoming responsive to properties of the material, entering into an ongoing dialogue with it, students are just implementing fixed ideas and might as well be using any material. He wants them to avoid naively underestimating the material's importance, which is typical of a beginning student. "They just happened to be in ceramics, so they're making this thing out of clay. But there's no reason for it to be made out of clay." This is the kind of thinking he wants students to avoid and to begin to understand how the clay is a partner in their creations.

More advanced students also have the same difficulty working with the properties of the clay. After Jason described one student's growing frustration and difficulties, he added,

Sometimes you just can't do certain things because the materials you have won't work the way you want them to. One point I was trying to make to her is that she might not have to actually follow her design exactly, and she might have to allow the process to be more fluid.

Students vary in the ease with which they develop techniques such as centering. As Jason noted, "It takes some students weeks and weeks and weeks until they can do that." He added that sometimes he spends class time mainly going around the room individually helping those students, demonstrating to them, and correcting their technique individually.

The teaching of craft is often central to visual arts classes. Technique is not something that constrains. Rather, acquiring technique gives students control over their works. And as students acquire technique, they begin to "think" with technique. Although technique was emphasized as an intended learning goal for every class we observed, we never saw technique being taught alone. As students learned some kind of technical skill they were also learning one or more of the other studio habits of mind. As students mastered perspective, for instance, they had to Observe and Envision; as they mastered shading, students became better able to Express the effects and emotional qualities of lighting; as students worked through color mixing, they had to Engage and Persist, frequently needing to manage frustration. Color mixing also allowed them to stretch and explore as they played and experimented. And of course the more they came to understand various techniques and studio practices, the better they could grasp the artist's world.

In the next chapter we look at how the art class teaches students to work through frustration, to not give up, to persist and remain engaged.

SIX

Learning to Engage and Persist

COMMITTING AND FOLLOWING THROUGH

I think they learned how to work through frustration.

—Kathleen Marsh

Teachers in rigorous visual arts classes present their students with engaging projects, and they teach their students to connect to the assignment personally, to persist in their work, and to stick to a task for a sustained period of time. Even 9th-graders began to internalize the culture of hard work. One 9th-grader at the Boston Arts Academy told us why he practices his drawing every day outside of class. "You can't expect to be great at it without practicing."

Students are taught to focus, to develop mental states conducive to working, and to develop inner-directedness. They are taught to break out of ruts and blocks, and to feel encouraged about their learning so that they are motivated to go on. When students are truly engaged, they lose themselves in concentration, forgetting about time, fully focused on the moment. They are in a state of "flow" (Csikszentmihalyi, 1990).

The primary means of teaching students to *Engage and Persist* is to present them with projects that are deeply engaging. All of the teachers we studied did this, as do excellent art teachers everywhere. But we were also struck by how often teachers spoke to students explicitly so as to keep them on track, to keep them engaged. Sometimes they did this by reminding students to stay focused (e.g., "pay attention," "get back on track"). At other times, teachers might help students sustain an experimental attitude rather than rush to a premature solution, as in this discussion between Jason and a student in the initial stages of envisioning her "unit sculpture."

Jason: Before you start that, I want you to think about the little coil, think about that and think about other forms or shapes of clay that you might use rather than just that little coil—maybe three or four different pieces of clay that you could repeat to build. . . .
Student: So you don't want me to do the pine cones?
Jason: I didn't say that.
Student: You want me to experiment first.
Jason: First, yes, rather than just starting, I want you to experiment with some different types of units. Some might be very geometric, some you might just grab and shape in your hand quickly.

Sometimes the teachers simply encouraged and praised the student's efforts (e.g., "you're doing a great job here"). Still other times, this goal takes the form of either creating tension by urging the student to keep going (e.g., playing energetic music; saying "don't stop now, keep at it"; or "you have only a half hour left to work"), or reducing tension, by, for example, playing relaxing music to help students focus. Thus, there are many routes to the goal of teaching students to Engage and Persist.

Typical comments that we coded as teaching to the goal of Engage and Persist included *keep going, work through the difficult part, focus, I know this is not easy,* and *be patient.*

In what follows, we present two classroom examples in which we see students working on projects that require sustained attention and motivation. In both classes, students wrestle with frustration and must work hard over time to meet a deadline.

DESIGNING IN CLAY:
COMPLETING THE TILE PROJECT   (EXAMPLE 6.1)

Toward the end of the school year at Walnut Hill, students are hard at work on a tile project in Jason Green's ceramic sculpture course. This project requires considerable technical skill and the willingness to stick to a task for several weeks without being able to see the end product. In an earlier class (see Example 7.2), students have designed a grid composed of nine tiles, and today their task is to finish their tiles. Students are asked to think about the shape, color, and texture of their tiles and to use the grid as a sketchbook in which they experiment with design options. As students come into class, they know what they are working on and go right to work. Jason calls this a "working class" (see Figure 6.1).

Students-at-Work

Today students must keep working hard if they are to finish the assignment by the deadline. "We will actually try to finish these tiles today, and that's a lot of work for some of you," Jason says, acknowledging that the students have a difficult task ahead of them.

Jason consults with students as they work, helping them focus on their work and stick to the task:

- *Stick to what you've begun.* Jason opposes a student's plan to start over, urging her to stick to the work she has begun. He also reminds her there is a deadline: "It won't be done by the show. That's all I can say if you want to start a new one. I would finish this."
- *Slowing down is sometimes a form of persisting.* To another student, Jason says, "So you just need to relax and take your time and build it."
- *Even if you're not happy with your work right now, it's important to keep going.* When a student says she feels her work looks "stupid," Jason gives her courage to keep on going. "You shouldn't be critical at this point, because it's so early in the process."
- *Learn to manage time as you work.* Jason suggests to a student that she find time to come to the studio outside of class so she can finish. He reminds her that she should glaze soon. "It's going to take you a while to glaze those pieces, I think. So you want to make some time in your schedule. This weekend. Friday."

- *Keep going even when you may not feel like it.* Jason tells a student to keep on going, even if she is not in the mood. "You should try to finish this today even if you don't feel like doing it. It's your last chance to get it done."

Jason Reflects

In our initial interview with Jason, he talked about how the medium of ceramics requires self-discipline because the material is continually changing and always drying out.

> I think it helps students develop habits—speedier habits that hopefully will allow or force them to think about things—and think about their artwork a little bit when they're outside of the classroom, so they don't just leave and forget about it. They have to remind themselves—you know, think about it sometimes. . . .

In our interview following this class, Jason talked about how students learn by following through, even if they don't like what they have made. By going through the process and coming up with something, students realize that not everything works.

Sometimes a class is just about working until the job is done. Jason characterized this class as a "working class" and the last "wet day," so students needed to get right to work.

> Just get work done so that we can finish things up. The goal was to . . . really get people to make decisions about things and do it . . . and that's . . . how art works when you have a deadline. And you know sometimes that's a good thing because you know your process is accelerated a little bit and you know you might have to make a quick decision or it changes the pace a little bit. So . . . that's sort of the overall goal [of this class] . . . do the work that needs to be done.

Jason also noted that students come to understand that art projects require work over extended periods of time. At the same time, there needs to be an emphasis on the way the program is set up.

> That's why we have 3-hour classes and . . . open studios on the weekends. . . . Here kids can just come in and work. . . . Time is such an important factor in doing what we do [and giving] the

Figure 6.1. Engage and Persist—Jason Green Helps Students Work on a Project That Lasts Several Weeks

A. Jason Green urges a student to continue the work she has begun

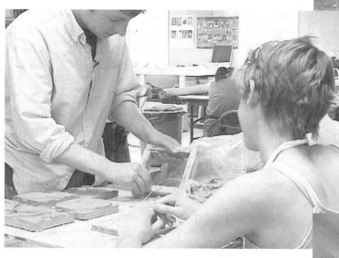

B. Jason's students go right to work as they enter class

C. Jason advises a student not to judge her work so early in the process of making ceramic art

D. Jason urges a student to try to finish by the end of class as he consults about her design decisions

students enough time to make these things that we ask them to make.

Jason acknowledged that this was a frustrating project, and students would never have completed it if they had not been pushed to persist. He added:

> The students didn't like the project very much, but they liked the results a lot. Almost across the board I think they were really frustrated with the whole thing, because they had to use so many tools and measure things, and I think they just really had to struggle a little bit, and, also, we had a short time line.

FINISHING THE PROCESS: MAKING PUPPETS PROJECT   (EXAMPLE 6.2)

As the final project in Kathleen Marsh's fall term, 9th-grade foundations class at the Boston Arts Academy, students are working on 3D projects. They have learned to encase an egg in a package strong enough to keep it from breaking when dropped 100 feet (see Example 12.7). This was followed by a joinery workshop with Barrington Edwards, a colleague in the visual art department at the Boston Arts Academy. In the class featured here, students are in the midst of work on a culminating project designed jointly by Kathleen and Barrington: making a 3D puppet with two kinds of joints and five moveable parts. Kathleen and Barrington have stressed the importance of linking craft and design in building the puppets, a technically demanding project.

Just as Jason recognized the difficulty of the multistep Tile Project, Kathleen is well aware of how challenging the multistep Puppet Project is. Students have told her that they are frustrated because their puppets look unfinished. They have not yet gotten them to the envisioned endpoint. Like Jason, she feels the need to encourage the students so that they will stay engaged. For example, at one point she asks, "How many of you feel frustrated with your pieces right now?" Many students raise hands. Her next comments offer encouragement:

> I want to say for all of you that you've done an amazing job. . . . To take something [paper] that's inherently two-dimensional and make it three-dimensional is really difficult. This is a really hard thing we're asking you to do. And you're doing a really good job. So, don't lose heart, OK?

As in Jason's class, students are working against a deadline, and they know that they are expected to persist in this project in out-of-class time. Kathleen reminds students of the deadline and suggests one way they might meet it:

> You . . . only have today to work on these. . . . You may stay after school. . . . I've been sad to see that only a few people have stayed after. These three girls have stayed after yesterday, but I haven't seen many people stay after school since we began talking about this deadline, which was quite a while ago.

Students are given clear information about just what they need to do to finish this project, to help them stick to the task by making it clear what the task demands. "I hear a lot of extra conversation. I know you guys are really ready to begin, OK? And I know you are really antsy, but I want to make sure that everybody is clear about what's required."

Kathleen also reminds students of expectations, "Part of the culture of this school, and not just this department, is that there is an expectation that you are going to spend time outside of class on your work." At the same time, she tells students why there is this expectation:

> Our expectation is that you spend a little time outside of school working on things, because we do want you to challenge yourself. We do want you to go above and beyond the very basics of what we ask, and sometimes that requires more time. OK? So, sometimes you need to get into the habit and culture of staying after school.

She reminds them that all of the visual arts teachers are available in the classrooms Monday through Thursday after school.

Students-at-Work

As students work, Kathleen offers encouragement to both individuals and to the whole class.

- *Don't give up. You've done a good job.* As she helps students, Kathleen pushes and encourages at the same time. She looks at one student's sketch and prods the student to continue. "Where are your moveable parts?" "You have a lot of work to do, but you have a good start. You've got to really focus." At the same time, she offers praise for what the student has done so far.

- *Remember the task at hand.* As Kathleen walks to help a student, she express her concern for the way the whole class is starting to lose focus, "I'm very worried by you. You're all over the place, and you're not focused."
- *Re-engage with a "good-enough" vision and a feasible plan of action you can carry through.* As Kathleen pauses to help a student joining paper strips, she offers advice:

> Don't fall in the trap of having a vision that's so far away that you can't satisfy the basics of the assignment, and don't get so caught up in disappointment that it's not matching your original vision. You and many others like you fall into that trap, and one of the things an artist needs to learn is that sometimes you just have to meet deadlines and meet the criteria being asked for rather than being too perfectionist.

Kathleen and Students Reflect

In an interview after the class, Kathleen reflected on the project and on helping students to Engage and Persist. Some students need to be monitored so that they stay on track. Others Engage and Persist on their own, yet even these independent students need to be checked in a large class so they don't get lost. "You have to keep checking everybody. Making sure they're still all going in the right direction. Making sure they're not losing focus, and it's hard 'cause that class is really big."

Kathleen finds that students at the Boston Arts Academy need support to stay focused, because

> A lot of kids who come to this school do not have the kind of external support that kids who are middle-class or upper-class have. Whether it's two parents. Whether it's money, whether it's experiences, they just don't have those opportunities, so we have to . . . create structure and support.

She finds that students learn to stay on task for increasingly longer periods of time. "I noticed that their attention span is lengthening. They're learning to work in longer studio sessions. They aren't asking me for breaks anymore."

One senior said learning to persist in work was the most important thing she learned in her 4 years at the Boston Arts Academy.

> Here they force you to stick with a piece. . . . I remember in middle school you just started drawing something, you just leave it on the table and walk away. You don't have to finish it like that. And I had a real difficult problem with sticking to my work because . . . I'd have an idea and I'd be all happy about it and I'd start it. And then by midway, I'd have another idea. And I'd get the idea from the piece that I started and so I'd just digress again and start over. And they had no problem with that in middle school. It's only like keeping you busy. It doesn't matter what you're doing. Then I got here. It was only Boston Arts Academy when I really started finishing pieces and that was a big thing for me because it's like wow, I actually completed something! And I like it! [*laughing*] So it was huge, it was like a big deal for me just to finish the work [see Figure 6.2].

A senior at Walnut Hill talks about her persistence and shows us how sticking to a project also involves the habit of *Envision*: The end product that she holds in her mind motivates her to keep working:

Figure 6.2. Charcoal Self-Portrait by a Senior at the Boston Arts Academy

I choose these methods of creating things that are so repetitive . . . I'll get halfway finished, and I'll just be like, "ugh, I don't want to do this anymore," but when I get to that point I'll look at what I've done, and I'll just think, "Oh this looks so cool, it will look so good once it's finished." So that's what gets me through it, just thinking about what the end product is going to look like [see Figure 6.3].

In our final interview with Kathleen, she talks about the importance of passion, which we see as the high end of engaging and persisting:

The thing that we talk a lot about as a school is that other thing that you look for, which is the unmeasurable thing, which we call "it," or "the twinkle in the eye," "the hunger," "the desire," and we don't measure it. We certainly talk about it, we certainly note it, we do write about it, but we don't measure it. There is no way to measure it.

Both Jason's Tile Project and Kathleen's Puppet-Making Project challenged students and grabbed their interest. The projects were within the students' abilities yet were novel and exciting. The projects also gave plenty of space for students to take a personal approach to the task. Teachers often played the role of gently keeping students on task and making sure they persisted in their engagement.

Figure 6.3. Wood Sculpture by a Senior at Walnut Hill

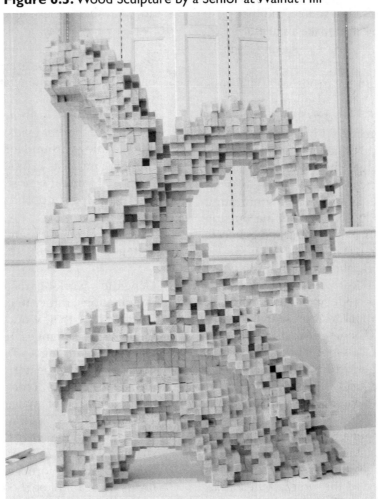

SEVEN

Learning to Envision

PLANNING BEYOND SEEING

I try to get them to think about how they would choose an object as a source, and then abstract from that object to make a sculpture.

—Jason Green

Students learn to *Observe* in visual arts classes (see Chapter 9), but they also learn to use observation as a springboard to *Envisioning* what they cannot observe directly with their eyes. Envisioning includes the acts of generating mental images so that one can imagine how a work will look, and planning ways to achieve that image. *Observing* and *Envisioning* are ends of the same continuum. When we observe, we look closely at the outside world. When we envision, we imagine and generate images of possibilities in our mind.

In observational work, the continuum between Observe and Envision is clear: we observe the model, and we represent that model in another medium. The translation from model to representation cannot be done without envisioning. Artists aim to represent not only the surface aspects of their models, but also the underlying structure or geometry—for example, the axis of the head versus the axis of the body, the torso as a trapezoid, the triangular relation between two figures.

In work that is not done from observation, the continuum is less clear, but it also exists. Artists work from mental images that are themselves derived from having observed the world. A freshman at Walnut Hill shows a developing ability to envision how what he observes can be altered to develop an expressive goal of bringing the focus to the small figures in the center of a drawing (see Figure 7.1).

Talking about an observational drawing of students standing at their easels, he explains how he did not draw just what he saw.

> Well, when I did the drawing it was supposed to be about the way the whole room looks and the way everything just comes in to the subjects. But there are a lot of . . . things around that would distract from what I was trying to draw. So I did change things around a little bit. I tried to make things as much as I could *point* to the middle here. . . . I think it's mostly the stuff that I left out that helps support the piece [see Figure 7.1].

Here are some of the many ways students were encouraged to *Envision*

- Generate a work of art solely from their imaginations, rather than from observation.
- Imagine how their work would look if they made specific changes. Here, the skill of *Envision* is used in planning a work.
- Make a "unit," repeat it, and then combine the units into sculptural forms. This is an example of another kind of envisioning focused on "improvisational" planning.
- Imagine all of the ways they can vary a line, a shape, a color, or a composition.
- Imagine implied forms in their drawings— forms that cannot be seen in full because they are partially occluded.
- Observe the underlying geometry of a form and then envision how that geometry can be shown in their work.

Figure 7.1. Charcoal Drawing of a Studio Class by a Freshman at Walnut Hill

Two classes are featured in this chapter, and both demonstrate two kinds of *Envisioning*—imagining and planning. Imagining is an activity that is required for planning a work, and it can be done in a host of ways.

PLACES FOR AN IMAGINARY CREATURE: INVENTING COLORS PROJECT   (EXAMPLE 7.1)

At the Boston Arts Academy near the conclusion of Beth Balliro's spring term course with 9th-graders, we see students continuing to work on the Imaginary Creatures Project. They are using acrylics to paint a mythical creature situated in the landscape in which it was born or died (see also Examples 5.1 and 13.1). The creature cannot be seen; thus it is envisioned.

Students-at-Work

As students work (see Figure 7.2), Beth repeatedly finds ways to focus students on one form of Envisioning—generating images from the imagination:

- *Imagine where your creature came from and create a landscape for the creature.* Beth asks a student to think explicitly of what he is trying to represent. "Wherever you think that beautiful creature can burst out of a seed. Where would it be? . . . a greenhouse, or a pot, or a windowsill, a crack in the sidewalk."
- *Create an imaginary landscape that tells a narrative.* Beth tells a student:

  > I want you to think about how you can tell a story with your landscape. I'm having you come up with where they were born, because to do that you will have to . . . have in mind a place and not use characters to show it. . . . I want you to have a landscape that has a story, and, in this case, I want you to think more deeply about your character.

- *Envision where the light is coming from in the landscape.* Beth asks a student to think about light. "Where is the light in this forest coming from . . . day or night? What time of day? What kind of light? Is it foggy? Bright and shining?" Beth also asks students to look closely at their work (Observe) as they plan, to see how it might grow (Envision).
- *Determine where on the page a new color could be used.* Beth asks a student, "Think about if there is a place where you want to include a color that's different than these."
- *Envision variations of a color.* Beth prods a student working with two colors to envision more variations of the colors. "OK, so you have red plus yellow . . . you have orange, think about how many oranges you can get."
- *Think of how to make color translucent and layered.* Beth asks students to think about how to layer colors "so you can still see the value shining through."

Beth Reflects

When asked to give this class a title, Beth called the class "Inventing Colors." As explained in Chapter 5, students were learning to envision new colors out of primaries, motivated by their struggles to envision a mythical creature that could in some way represent themselves, in landscapes of its birth and death. When asked why students should learn to invent rather than copy, Beth replied that when students just follow tradition, their work is "so

Figure 7.2. Envision—Beth Balliro and Her Students Consider Ways to Paint Environments Where Imaginary Creatures Lived

A. Beth Balliro works on color with her students

B. Beth and a student consider how a landscape expresses character

C. Beth urges a student to envision how to vary the color

D. Beth wonders with a student how to expand the range of colors in a work

much less interesting than when they invent. So, that's why I didn't want to lead them by requiring that they look at references." Beth also thinks it's important to have students learn the relationship between drawing from imagination and drawing from observation because "fantasy drawings will be much better if you work on observation" (see Figure 7.3).

Figure 7.3. Sun Painting by a 9th-grader at the Boston Arts Academy

DESIGNING IN CLAY:
BEGINNING THE TILE PROJECT   (EXAMPLE 7.2)

In Jason Green's classroom at Walnut Hill, students are beginning a tile project near the end of their second-semester course in ceramics. In this class, they are assigned to create nine tiles pressed from molds. They place objects into the molds to press out individual textured tiles. They must think of each tile in relation to the whole, as in painting, because the nine tiles, each 5-inches square, must form a piece that can be hung on the wall (see also Example 6.1).

Students-at-Work

As students work, Jason frequently asks them to envision the next steps in their work. Below are Jason's interactions with two students as he prods both to think of what they might do next with their work:

- *How might individual tiles function as a single piece?* Jason tells a student, "I want you to think of how the tiles relate. Have something that

connects them together between the tiles." To another, he says, "You need to know what each tile will look like before you start making it." He further warns her to avoid carving all nine pieces separately; she will need to think in terms of a grid.

- *What would your work look like if you tried something else?* Jason asks the student to think of the basic things that make up the design. He then asks her, "What would happen if you did it on each tile, so you didn't have to carve nine pieces of plaster?" (This also nurtures the Studio Habit of Mind Stretch and Explore, because Jason is encouraging the student to consider options.)

- *What do you plan to do?* Jason asks a student what she plans: "You have to decide if you want the middle out, coming closer to you. That means you will have to cut these little squares."

- *What technique might you employ?* As the student struggles with her grid drawing, Jason suggests that she think of how she might execute what she plans: "You could cut something like this [he picks up a straight piece of wood] and have it go into the mold, and you would get a nice straight line."

Jason Reflects

In an interview after this class, Jason noted that this project requires advanced planning, which we refer to as Envisioning. "They're making all the decisions about their artwork when they're not actually working on the clay." He also stressed that in this project, students have to "figure out" ahead of time (Envision) the end product before beginning to build the object.

Jason said his goal was to have students envision their own product and not follow a set of automatic steps: "What I don't want to do is give them the recipe for making art, because there is no real recipe." Instead, Jason's goal is to help students find their own solutions: "I want to give them the tools so that they can be innovators and come up with their own problems and their own solutions and their own questions."

One might at first think that Envisioning occurs only when artists work from imagination. But Envisioning also occurs when working from the model or when combining imagination and observation in works. Every time artists plan next steps they are

Envisioning. Every time they step back and ask themselves how the work would look if they made some kind of alteration they are Envisioning. The teachers asked students to plan and to imagine revisions in their works. Thus students gained considerable practice in working from mental images. Envisioning—the ability to imagine and to generate mental images—is a disposition important in many domains. And visual arts classes are perhaps the arenas in which this disposition is most consistently fostered and demanded.

In the next chapter we consider how students learn to go beyond technique to express a personal vision in their work.

EIGHT

Learning to Express

FINDING PERSONAL VISIONS

The strength of the drawing is going to depend very much on the evocative nature of the space.

—Jim Woodside

In visual arts classes, students are taught to go beyond technical skill to convey a personal intention in their work. Learning to *Express* includes making works that exemplify properties that are not literally present, such as moods, sounds, and atmosphere. Learning to Express also means making works that convey properties such as emotions, a sense of movement, or personal meaning.

In the following two classes, we see students learning different aspects of expression. In both, we see examples of class structures and interactions with students that encourage them to go beyond representation to create something with evocative meaning.

DRAWING FOR FEELING: FIGURES IN EVOCATIVE SPACE PROJECT (EXAMPLE 8.1)

At Walnut Hill in Jim Woodside's Figures in Evocative Space Project (see also Examples 12.1 and 15.2), students learn to convey a mood or atmosphere in their drawing that evokes something about the psychology of the figures in the drawing. Jim moves students away from thinking about representing a single figure, as they had in previous classes, toward thinking about figures in relationship, telling a story in an evocative space (see Figure 8.1).

Demonstration–Lecture

Five months into his drawing class, Jim introduces his students to the concept of drama and narrative. He poses a male and female student together at opposite sides of a space. He asks the rest of the students to think of the models as kids just hanging out. He contrasts this kind of drawing with more standard fare in which he asks students to draw an isolated figure he has set up for them and makes comments, such as those that follow, encouraging them to be expressive in their drawings.

- *Jim asks students to use drawing to express a dramatic relationship.*

   I'm trying to set up a kind of dramatic lighting . . . a lighting that seems almost mysterious or evocative. . . . I want this to be set up like a kind of stage. . . . You know, when you think of actors on a stage, you don't just think of the personalities, but you think of the whole story being told. You think of the lighting. You think of the kind of environment being implied, right?

- *Jim asks students to think about what is implied, suggesting that they think as if they were movie directors and show their decisions in their drawings:*

   These two people are elements in a drama. . . . What I'm asking you to do is move beyond the idea of just drawing a figure in an art class, which is what we've done for

Figure 8.1. Express—Jim Woodside's Students Learn to Express Emotional Content in Their Figure Drawings

A. Jim Woodside focuses students' attention on light as a source of drama in drawings

B. Jim's students begin drawing figures in dramatic lighting

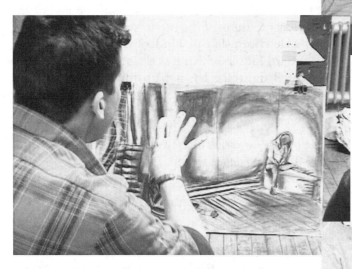

C. Jim leads a critique

D. Jim encourages an uncertain student to heighten contrast in his drawing to show the dramatic relationship between the figures

the last couple of weeks. Now I'm asking you to think more about the emotional content, the relationship between the two, the drama, the mystery.

- *Jim asks students to Express the relationship between the two figures in the empty space between them:*

    You're going to have to include all this space, this empty space. Now that's going to be a big challenge in your drawing, because something is going to be in that space, you know? There's gonna' be the wall, the blackness of the window, but more importantly, what's the sort of emotional content and character, and what do you get out of that drawing? Let me rephrase that—the strength of the drawing is going to depend very much on the evocative nature of this space.

Jim also introduces paintings by Edward Hopper and Richard Deibenkorn and leads a discussion about these paintings' evocative, emotional content (see Example 12.1). In addition to his focus on *Express*, he fosters students' Understanding of the Art World as the students learn how their work relates to that of professional artists. He helps them *Observe*, as students learn to see light and value by looking closely at works of art, and he asks them to *Question and Explain*, as they are asked to describe qualities in the work.

Students-at-Work

Jim consults with students as they work on a series of quick, compositional sketches (3–5 minutes each), and then on a longer drawing on better paper:

- *Notice the expressive light on the face of the female model.* Jim directs a student's attention to the strong, very clear light on one side of the model's face and the dark values on the other, and says, "That can be all the information you need. A sort of very mysterious, wonderful light across one side of her body." This consult also fosters learning to Observe as the student is shown how to look closely at the model.
- *Create a dramatic sense of receding space by exaggerating perspective.* Jim puts tracing paper on the drawing to demonstrate as he suggests to a student that he include in his drawing pictures on the wall "because if you put them on in perspective, it's the perfect way of telling the viewer that the space is going back. But you can make that even more dramatic if you like, exaggerating the diminishing side of the picture." This consult also fosters the learning of Develop Craft: Technique, as the student is encouraged to use the rules of perspective learned earlier in the semester, and the learning of Observe, as the student is encouraged to notice space around the models and use it to express an intended effect.
- *Use the technique of erasing to convey a dramatic feeling of light.* Jim suggests that a student use the technique of erasing. "This drawing is the type of drawing that sort of works from darkness backward instead of putting darkness on." He also asks the student to recall a project from several months ago, when he covered the paper in charcoal and erased into it (see Example 4.3). "In a way, there's a similar thing going on here, where bits of light are worked out of darkness." Jim asks for permission to erase the student's drawing a bit and describes what he's doing. "In certain areas where it's important to show the weight of the figure, go back in with your eraser. You know, heighten that contrast in certain areas." This consult also fosters the learning of Develop Craft: Technique, and is a good example of how students are taught to be alert to craft (and develop technical skill) in the service of expression.

Critique

During the class, Jim uses several short Critique sessions to point out how specific compositional decisions determine the kind of relationship conveyed between the two figures. Students' works, taped onto drawing boards, are leaned informally against the wall for all to sit before and contemplate. Jim praises students' success at making decisions in their sketches about what they want to express. In discussing the drawings, he directs students' attention to expression as "powerful decisions starting to be made, starting to emerge out of your sketches."

During the Critique, Jim notes how one student has created a strong statement of isolation by the choices made. He points to small, discrete figures and suggests the power of really exaggerating the distance between them. "Maybe it's a statement about the lack of communication between the two figures."

Jim further compares the expression of the deep space in the drawing to another student's drawing that is flatter. He points out how the dramatic angle gives the picture a less stable effect, and the result of the student's choice to include architectural elements such as the wall and the floor, information which Jim says is really the substance of the drawing. "It's not a portraiture, it's just arrangement of shapes."

Jim also shows the class a finished drawing of the same kind of scene by a student in another class to explain what he means by telling a story. He points out the power of the open space and the way the drawing is done with just a hint of light around the otherwise anonymous figure. Finally, he comes back to the idea of a stage set. "When I talk about telling a story, I'm not saying that you're illustrating an event, a story, but I'm saying that you're implying a drama, a sort of living drama between figures."

Jim Reflects

In our interviews with Jim, he talked about how he strives to teach students to find personal relationships in their art and how he never teaches technique alone. "It is about connecting the art to your life and to the world, and your place in the world." Jim talked about why he never wants to teach just skills and then go on to content and expression. "It is not [only] the skill of drawing that they are learning. It is very much the making of a mark in the world as expression; and, to me, that might be something that is more interesting and more exciting for them."

For Jim, the teaching of technique is only part of the picture. "I have had kids in drawing that could draw better than I could, but they really couldn't push it to another level. There is just not depth in their work." He tries to help students see how an idea, like drawing the figure, connects to a world that they relate to and understand. "Whether it's them with their parents in the kitchen or whether it's kids hanging out in Harvard Square, there's a kind of drama to everyday life." And what hits you first when you look at a work of art is not its technique but its evocative properties.

In our final interview with Jim as he reflected on the year, he said that the assignments do get more interpretative as he moves through the year. They are more evocative in terms of expression, but he stressed that expression cannot be conceived of in isolation from other aspects of drawing.

DRAWING FOR MEANING: IMAGINARY CREATURES PROJECT   (EXAMPLE 8.2)

At the Boston Arts Academy, in Beth Balliro's Imaginary Creatures Project in the middle of her second-semester course with 9th-graders, she stressed that students should express personal meaning in their work. The students are each making a mythical creature that expresses something about their own personality. They are going beyond representation to create something with connotative, evocative meaning. In an earlier class, students wrote about what inspires them ("What is your muse?"); (see Example 10.1). Now with this inspiration in mind, Beth helps them to do a pencil sketch in which they think of themselves as a mythical creature—part human, part animal. As students worked, Beth encouraged them to identify properties through which to convey personal meaning in two ways:

- *Decide which aspects of character to express in the mythical figure.* Beth asks a student several questions to get him to think about which aspects of his character he wants to express in his mythical figure. "If you could be any character, would this be the one? A warrior? What about you is the most dominant part of you?" Beth also reassures the student that he is already steps ahead in the challenge of making a drawing that synthesizes man and beast. Now he has to make sure he is ready to commit to this drawing as the basis for a big painting later.
- *Decide how your drawing will express that character.* Beth urges a student to put her figure of a mermaid into action so that it expresses more power, and so that the mermaid expresses something about the student's self. She encourages the student to make "not just any old mermaid but your own mermaid. . . . Instead of having a portrait of a mermaid, see if you can put it in action." When the student responds that mermaids have power over the waves, Beth replies, "Yes, so that tells part of her power."

Beth and a Student Reflect

In an interview, Beth talked about how she was indirectly trying to influence the student who chose to make a mermaid—trying to get her to think about the viewer and make a creature that conveys something to that viewer. Although she really didn't want the student to do a mermaid, she didn't want to tell her not to do a mermaid because the student was invested in a lot of draft drawings of mermaids, and "she was pretty psyched up about the mermaid thing. But in my mind I'm thinking, uhh, a mermaid!" Beth wanted the student to avoid being "clichéd":

Art that is clichéd doesn't engage the viewer, and art that presents something intriguing does engage the viewer. So, I don't know that she's ever thought about the viewer before. I'm trying to get her to see the work outside of herself as something that conveys something to a viewer.

A senior at Walnut Hill talked to us about how she learned to go beyond technique and realism, and began to use her skills in representation for an expressive and personal aim.

I came . . . to this school and I basically just was thinking about skill and showing skill and you know trying to create depths and dimension and just show what's real and show that I can present it in a real way. And that's the perfect example [apple drawing]. . . . But with my self-portrait, it clearly shows how I'm more . . . working with myself and . . . who I am. . . . It's very personal, it's more deep, and it's not about presenting something in a realistic way. . . . It still has a lot of skill in it. . . . But the whole general idea of what I'm trying to present has changed. And I grew a lot through that because basically when I came here I started to have a lot of skill but I didn't really know what to do with it or how to connect it with my thinking (see Figure 8.2).

In our initial interview, Beth told us why learning to be expressive is so important for her students. "They have equally not really found their voice, in a way that it can be heard. I think being an artist is figuring out how to get yourself heard." In a later interview, Beth talked about how it is that students can discover their voice in an art class but still struggle in an academic class. Here she has brought up the vexing issue of transfer. Whether students can discover their voice (and thus something about their identity) in an arts class and have this discovery generalize outside of art class is a question ripe for investigation.

Figure 8.2. Self-Portrait by a Senior at Walnut Hill

NINE

Learning to Observe

SEEING BEYOND THE ORDINARY

Keep investigating things around you. . . . Looking is the real stuff about drawing.

—Mickey Telemaque

Students in the art studio are taught to look more closely than people ordinarily do. They learn to see with new eyes. They are helped to move beyond their habitual ways of seeing, to notice things that might otherwise be invisible and therefore not available as something to think about. This is the Studio Habit of careful, mindful Observation.

Students are taught to look closely at the following:

- The model or source from which they are working
- Their own artworks as they evolve
- Art processes modeled and artworks created by the teacher in demonstrations
- Artworks created by other students
- Artworks from contemporary or historical artists

Teachers help students notice more by pointing out nuances of color, line, texture, and form. They point out the underlying geometry of a form. They describe the expressive properties of a work, as well as its stylistic and compositional elements.

In the two classes that follow, we show how students are taught to observe. Both teachers have their students use a viewfinder (a small piece of cardboard with a rectangle cut out of its center), a tool artists have traditionally used to aid observation.

In Mickey Telemaque's first design class of the term at the Boston Arts Academy, students learn to look through a viewfinder with one eye, so that they can learn a new way of seeing—seeing the world as elements in a composition. He tells them, "Instead of painting what we see, we're going to see what you would paint." This is meant to help them select what they want to put on a page.

Demonstration–Lecture

Looking through the viewfinder helps students learn to see objects as only lines, shapes, and colors in a frame. Mickey tells students:

Forget that you are looking at a bucket or a person's hair, or a table and a chair, and all these things. Forget that these are objects that have any real definition. I want you to simply concentrate on the lines that are created . . . in what you see.

Mickey talks about what he sees when looking through the viewfinder. He turns and holds the viewfinder up to a desk.

Right here I am paying attention particularly to the way this line goes diagonally across this frame, and then there is another little line underneath it that I can see has a little bit of a distance. It's a different color, different texture, and the line is thicker because from my perspective this line is a little thinner than this line down here.

Mickey explains how, when you look through a viewfinder with one eye, you lose depth perception and start to see the world as if it were a two-dimensional picture. Instead of seeing one thing in front of another "all you're seeing is [that] one thing stops where another thing starts. And that is all design, because one color in a shape stops and the other starts."

Students-at-Work

Mickey hands out viewfinders, and students practice seeing the world as design (see Figure 9.1). As they look around the classroom and hallway, Mickey keeps students focused on this new way of seeing by engaging in observations with them. Mickey asks individual students, groups of students, and sometimes the whole class to do the following:

- *Vary how the tool is used.* Mickey explains what to notice when looking through the viewfinder with one eye. "Think about how things look different when you hold it close to your eye or closer to the object."
- *Focus on design elements.* Mickey asks students to forget what they are looking at and just think about the surfaces.

> Is anybody having trouble forgetting that they're looking at something that they already know? . . . Forget that you're looking at somebody's arm or a table. Just think about the shapes, the colors, the lines, and the textures and the value of things as they change as you move the viewfinder around.

- *Notice, think, and respond.* Mickey asks students to talk about what they see differently by using the viewfinder: "Do you notice something that you're not used to paying attention to?"

Demonstration–Lecture

After students have investigated the classroom and hallway, Mickey gathers them in the classroom and uses a magazine cover with an image of a building and a poster on the wall to help synthesize what

they've learned—paintings don't have to be seen as what they represent; rather, they can be seen as simply a surface of colors, shapes, patterns, textures, and forms. "That little change in thinking is what I want you to concentrate on." Mickey concluded by introducing a homework assignment that connected the "new way of looking" to the course focus on design: Students created sheets of numerous thumbnail sketches that each combined one circle, triangle, and square, in an effort to find those designs that best conveyed the idea of motion.

Mickey Reflects

When we asked Mickey to give this class a title, he called it "A New Way of Seeing," or "Seeing the New." He explained that his goal is to "change how they look." "We're seeing what we are going to paint," Mickey says as an explanation for using the viewfinders.

The goal of looking more closely, Mickey explained to us, is to demystify the act of drawing and realize that the challenge of drawing a complex object is no different from the challenge of drawing a simple one.

> What happens is they think, "I can't draw a person." But if you say draw this pencil they probably won't say that. But really . . . the lines are just different. So make the line that corresponds to what you see. Turn it here. Shadow it here. It's stripping away what it is and just painting the lines.

Mickey is, in short, teaching students to look closely so that they can begin to draw what they never thought they could draw. The first step, he tells them, is to learn to see.

SEEING THE WORLD AND PUTTING IT ON PAPER: LIGHT AND BOXES PROJECT   (EXAMPLE 9.2)

For Jim Woodside's Light and Boxes Project at Walnut Hill, students learn to think about the relationship between the world and their drawing. Students use the viewfinder to see the world anew, and then go one step further and think about how they can put what they see onto paper.

Early in the fall semester, students file into Jim's classroom to find a pile of wooden and cardboard boxes in neutral tones stacked at a variety of angles in the center of the floor (see also Examples 4.3 and

Figure 9.1. Observe—Mickey Telemaque's Students Learn to See with "New Eyes"

A. Mickey Telemaque asks students to use a viewfinder to "see what you would paint"

B. Mickey guides students to see design in the environment outside the windows

C. Mickey tells students to forget that they're seeing objects and focus on just lines

D. Mickey explains that viewfinders help people see objects as just lines, shapes, and colors in a frame

5.3). The students gather around this unusual "still life," and Jim gives them each a viewfinder. As did Mickey, Jim teaches his students how the viewfinder helps them see, and as a result, helps them draw more accurately.

Demonstration–Lecture

Jim shows the students how to look through the viewfinder at the still life from many angles, and he explains how the viewfinder can help them decide about the composition of their drawings:

> This is a really great way to isolate what you want to work on to get a sort of preview of it, to figure out, most importantly, how it relates to all four sides of the paper. If you look through that you'll start to get a sense of, "Is there enough in that composition to occupy my drawing? Is there too much? Do I need to move in closer? Do I need to step back?"

Jim explains that students are also going to be working on perspective:

> We're still talking about line, but the main emphasis of what we're going to work on today is going to be perspective, geometry, one- and two-point perspective, how to arrange these shapes in a logical way, in a way that makes sense, in a way that is representative of the space that exists here in real life, on your two-dimensional surface.

Before students start drawing, Jim holds up the viewfinder and explains to the class how to use it to plan a composition:

> As you look through the viewfinder, look at all four sides. Don't just think of the top and then the bottom, you know, like we tend to look at the earth and think of the sky and the ground. Look at all four sides of the hole in the cardboard, because that's how you're going to start to think about all four sides of your piece of paper, in terms of the composition. Think about how the lines work, intersect, interact, with all four sides.

Students are given newsprint, tempera paint, and brushes as their drawing tools and materials. They are told to draw the outlines of the boxes only, and

to concentrate on how one form relates to another in space. "Learn to see shapes," Jim tells them.

Students-at-Work

Jim circulates, watches, asks questions, and encourages students to use the viewfinder. Occasionally he speaks to the whole group, but usually he talks to one student at a time. For example, Jim helps one student see the major vertical organizing lines that structure the still life. "Most of the things in the still life are set straight up and down, OK?" He also suggests what the student might do next:

> So if I were you, I would stop on this part right now and get some of these straight verticals in, like maybe that big pedestal there, or maybe that box down there if that's in your view . . . so you can work these big diagonals against that.

Critique

After students have made a preliminary drawing, Jim puts all the drawings up on the wall and holds the first Critique of the 3-hour class. He begins the Critique by asking students to look at their own drawing and think about what's *wrong* with it. The Critique moves fluidly into a Demonstration–Lecture.

Demonstration–Lecture

Using student drawings as a reference, Jim puts up a blank sheet of paper on which he draws boxes as he talks about principles of perspective drawing. He introduces some terms, writing them and illustrating them simply—horizon line (eye level), one-point perspective, vanishing point—and draws boxes in various positions above and below the horizon line. Jim shows students an old movie projector case and demonstrates how perspective helps to understand the simple overall shape of the case and to look beyond the minor details—handle, latch, etc. He explains why they should first draw the general shape of the rectangular projector case, and as he lifts the cover to reveal the projector itself, only later alter that same shape when depicting the specific details of the projector:

> Whether you're drawing a person or the most complicated thing in the world, you want to see it in simple terms first. It really helps to understand things in simple geometric terms first.

Jim makes a connection to the way he asks students to think of the figure:

> This is the same thing as when you draw a person. I'll tell you as we draw the figure to learn to break it up into geometry. If you just think of like the chest and muscles and arms and everybody's different shape, it can be overwhelming. But if you think of someone as just a cube and another cube attached, it can really help to simplify it.

Much of what we hear in this Demonstration–Lecture is similar to how Jim talked to individual students in teacher–student consults during the Students-at-Work session. But here, he talks to the entire group, making reference to individual students' works, thereby moving seamlessly back into Critique.

Critique

Before beginning another round of Students-at-Work, Jim helps students talk about what they see in their own and others' works that they think is more or less successful. Students discuss point of view in different drawings and the importance of intentionally choosing the point of view in a drawing. Jim concludes by telling students, "So these are the kind of thought processes and choices you should make with every single drawing."

Students-at-Work

Following the Critique, students return to working on the still life, this time drawing it armed with the rules of perspective. With one student, Jim demonstrates perspective drawing by placing a piece of tracing paper over the student's drawing and then drawing from the student's viewpoint. As he draws, Jim explains and points out to the student aspects of the display and how he is capturing these in the drawing. "Where is your horizon line?" he asks the student. To the student's reply he answers, "Right, so that means this is significantly below your horizon line, right? OK, so let's just say that the vanishing points are off here, they're somewhere but it's imaginary, off your piece of paper." Jim continues to draw and direct the student's attention to the drawing.

Jim also focuses the group's observation on other students' work. He holds up a drawing and directs

students to observe the expressive quality of charcoal in this work.

> She's got this beautiful, very hard angular drawing of the objects, OK? But for the interior it looks like she's just sort of pretty much rubbing her fingers in toward the inner shape, taking that charcoal and pushing it in. Pretty simple solution, but I think it comes up with a really powerful expressive result, don't you?

For a student who is really struggling, Jim demonstrates how to get the horizon line right by working directly on the student's drawing. While marking on students' work is controversial among art educators, Jim and his students share an understanding that this classwork is an exercise, not a work of art, and therefore, his marks do not violate the integrity of the students' expression. Nevertheless, Jim respectfully asks the students' permission before adding his own lines to the paper. Then, as he draws, he explains his marks:

> OK, where is your horizon line? Do you know? It's about right there, right? So why do you have these going up? I'm going to do it right over, OK? [*Drawing on student's drawing.*] Your horizon line is right there, OK? You'd see a little bit of the bottom, don't you? So if I'm looking at it, it's going be like this.

Jim and Students Reflect

In an interview, Jim spoke about some of the reasons he taught this class as he did. He explained that if you look through a viewfinder at the still life, "you're basically looking at an abstract piece of art" by becoming aware of all four sides of the piece of paper. "If you look through the viewfinder at a still life, which is just boxes and shapes, you become immediately aware of lines intersecting on all four sides." This is a complex way of looking at a work, and most students don't think that way "but the viewfinder helps them to and it's a great thing. It just gets the visual clutter out of their assignment."

The value of critiquing your own work is to help students learn to see and "to be able to look at your own work after you've done it and do more than just be pleased with yourself." In looking at the work of others, you learn. And posing a question for the group means each student had to think, "OK, I might get called on to say what is wrong with my picture. I better look at it and pay attention." In reflecting with us after class about the Critique, Jim explained, "I wanted them to look at their own drawings and analyze them in a right–wrong/yes–no fashion." This was not intended to be a deeper critique of their thinking and expression in their work. Students were simply to find a box that just didn't look right. The form that the Critique takes follows its purpose.

Jim explains how the goal of teaching perspective is to get students to see the simple geometry underlying the forms: "It's hard for kids to see things simple. I think that simplification is a goal in art." He explains,

> Brancusi, the sculptor, had this great quote that I might even have said to the kids, "Simplicity is complexity solved." It comes up in big sophisticated ideas in art and also in things like this. So when you draw the human figure I try to get them to see the form. It's the forest through the trees sometimes—you see the big picture.

When asked to give this class a title, Jim called it "Living Use of Perspective and Composition." He means to show students how the skill of perspective drawing can be used in all drawing—it is a way of grasping the architecture underlying form. In his post-class interview, Jim explained why he does not teach perspective just by having students draw a box in isolation, but rather asks them to Observe the principles of perspective in what they see. "By having them draw a whole still life, they're making a work of art. They're not just drawing a box and learning how to do it." By embedding the skill to be learned in the context of artistic challenges, students don't merely learn the skill itself, they learn to use the skills for their own purposes.

As students learn to see, their observational drawing skill improves. One 9th-grader at Walnut Hill realized how far he had come in his ability to Observe when he talked about his first still life. He told us why he thought the drawing was not accurately drawn: "I didn't really *look* at it. I just saw what I thought I saw and just drew. And I didn't really like break it down" (see Figures 9.2 and 9.3)

Figure 9.2. A 9th-Grader at Walnut Hill Explains That in His First Drawings He Drew "What I Thought I Saw"

Figure 9.3. Late in the 9th Grade, a Student Explains That He Looks More Carefully Now by "Breaking It Down"

Students carry the habit of Observation outside of the classroom. A Boston Arts Academy senior told us how she began to notice perspective in the environment after learning about it in an observational drawing class:

> I remember walking down Lansdowne Street. I looked at the way that the street goes in, and it's exactly what he was talking about how things fade into . . . space and it's a vanishing point at the end. . . . And I was like "OK, and so this art stuff does make sense." [I noticed it before] but I didn't understand why I saw it like that.

Even a beginning student noticed how he was starting to look at things differently. A 9th-grader at Walnut Hill commented on this: "When you're painting . . . it's an extremely different way of looking at things than when you're not. Because you see things, or at least I see things, in huge blocks of light and color. . . . You look at things differently."

Students who spend time in classrooms such as Mickey's and Jim's are getting continual eye training. There is looking, and then there is seeing. Students learn that looking is not always seeing. Their eyes are now opened. It is tempting to believe, but still in need of demonstration, that students who come out of such classrooms look more closely when they peer through a microscope in biology class, notice more aspects of a person's face that they want to describe in a creative writing project, and look more closely at the inside of a flower and notice its mathematical symmetry.

TEN

Learning to Reflect

THINKING METACOGNITIVELY

My goal . . . is to have them . . . question the way they do things. And lose bad habits and develop new good habits.

—Beth Balliro

I'm trying to . . . give them the questions that they should be asking themselves while they're making something. Or after they've made something.

—Jason Green

When we're talking about looking at artwork, whether it's one in the museum or your own or your classmate's, it's still that slowing process; it's still that trying to separate the difference between interpretation and description.

—Kathleen Marsh

In strong visual arts classes, students are asked to become reflective about their art-making, and this reflection takes two forms. They are asked to think about and explain their process, decisions, and intentions, a process we refer to as *Question and Explain*. And they are also asked to judge their own work and that of others, a process we refer to as *Evaluate*. Both of these dispositions involve the construction of meaning: Students think about their own artistic goals and those of others. Both also involve self-knowledge: Students learn about themselves and their reactions and judgments as they evaluate work, whether their own or that of others. And both involve consideration of quality: Describing work is prerequisite to evaluating elements of varying levels of effectiveness. Evalua-tion involves some kind of comparison of the work with other works or with the envisioned final work not yet achieved.

TEACHING STUDENTS TO QUESTION AND EXPLAIN

Teachers often ask students to step back and focus on an aspect of their work or working process, something that we believe occurs much more frequently in the art studio than in non-art classes. Often, teachers use questions as prompts to help students think about their work. We noticed teachers asking students to explain *what* some part of their drawing depicted (literally), *how* they had achieved a certain effect, *why* they made something the way they did, and *what* changes they were planning in their work. When teachers posed questions that could be answered with a simple yes or no, we did not consider these as prompting the habit of Questioning and Explaining. We saw open-ended questions that prompt students to reflect and explain aloud, or even silently to themselves, as evidence that teachers meant students to learn to Question and Explain. These kinds of questions help foster an inner voice of reflection in the language of words, in contrast to the visual symbols that students think with when they work with art tools and materials.

In the first two classes that follow, we show how students are taught to Question and Explain. In both these classes, teachers use questioning to help students focus on a particular aspect of their work and to reflect on what they are making and how they are working.

DRAWING YOURSELF AS MYTHICAL: IMAGINARY CREATURES PROJECT (EXAMPLE 10.1)

Near the middle of the second-semester class for 9th-graders at the Boston Arts Academy, students in Beth Balliro's class have recently visited the Boston Museum of Fine Arts. Beth talks about how a museum is a house of muses—and the muses are the keepers of the arts. Today students are asked to paint their muses—themselves as a mythical creature. The creature must be semihuman and must express something about the student's self. Students look at themselves in mirrors as they imagine their muse (see also Example 8.2).

Demonstration–Lecture

Beth first asks students to write about what inspires them. On the board she writes the following three questions for students to answer:

- What/who is your "muse?"
- If you had mythical powers, what would they be?
- What would your weaknesses be?

As she gets pens and brushes out, Beth pursues these questions with individual students. Next, she hands out ink and packets with photocopies of mythical creatures from African and Native American cultures that students can use to help them envision their creatures.

Students-at-Work

While students draw their mythical creatures, Beth circles from student to student, pressing them to explain how the character they are drawing in fact reflects something about themselves (see Figure 10.1). Here are some of the questions she asks students to encourage them to develop the habit of Question and Explain:

- How would this be you?
- What part of this character would be you looking in the mirror?
- How's it going to be you?
- Tell me about it. . . . How is he part you?
- What kind of character is this? Do you really want to be this character?
- And how is this you, the glasses and the eyes?

- So this is you plus what? You said some cat and what did you say? Some type of cat. . . . So how do the eyelashes make it seem half-human, half-animal?

Beth sometimes points to specific parts of a drawing and asks students to explain what they did or are trying to do there:

- So did you just use a brush?
- How did you get this detail? It's beautiful.
- Tell me about those ears.

Beth Reflects

In an interview after class, we asked Beth to say more about her questioning techniques. She talked about two ways to help students learn to Question and Explain: Asking students to answer their own questions for the next 10 minutes, and having students keep journals in which they write about process on a daily basis. In this class, though, she has a minimal goal in mind: getting students to talk about their art-making process. That seems clearly attainable for all her students and is a first, simple, and concrete step in their development.

The habit of reflection helps students become independent workers and become "able to self-monitor so that they can eventually be autonomous," Beth explains. She believes that becoming reflective can help art students gain confidence when they are in academic classes in which they may not be strong students. "I want them to be able to articulate their process and articulate how they're different from other students." They can "figure out how to be more of a presence and how to advocate for their own growth in a way that allows people to hear them."

Learning to be reflective about one's work and to advocate gives the emerging artist power in today's art world. "Part of their responsibility, I think, of being artists is figuring out how to get yourself heard."

BUILDING OBJECTS IN RELATION: COIL SCULPTURE PROJECT (EXAMPLE 10.2)

In Jason Green's Coil Sculpture Project near the start of the second term of ceramics at Walnut Hill, when the focus has shifted from wheel-throwing to sculpture, again we see students being asked to Question and Explain their work. Jason asks students to look around the room to find two objects

Figure 10.1. Reflect: Question and Explain—Students in Beth Balliro's Class Represent Aspects of Their Personalities in Mythical Creatures That They Create

A. Beth Balliro prompts a student to pause and think about his work

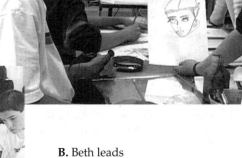

B. Beth leads students in reflecting on their visit to the museum—a "house of muses"

C. Beth guides students to reflect on their personal muses

D. Beth urges students to consider what personal characteristics they could emphasize in their mythical creatures

that could serve as the referents for a hand-built ceramic sculpture created with coil technique. The assignment is challenging because students are not to make a copy of the objects, but rather to create a new object that combines parts or all of the two objects they are using as models, varying scale as their intention dictates. Additionally, the sculptures must not have a flat bottom. The students are not making pottery, which is flat on one side so that it can stack on a shelf, but sculptures, which are built to be viewed from all sides. Students also have to make two experimental tiles with textures on them. From these tiles, they will choose the patterns that they want to use as the "skins" of their sculptures.

Students-at-Work

All of the techniques students have learned thus far will be used in this project. As students begin, Jason circles the room consulting with individual students.

- *Describe your plans.* "Do you know what you're going to do?" Jason asks a student as he prompts her to explain how she plans to use a light bulb. Later he returns to the same student to ask, "What about this form? What's the whole thing going to look like?" Jason questions another student to help her think how she might build with coils. "What's your object?" "Do you want to make the whole thing?" "Which part of it?"
- *Justify your choice as an aesthetic decision.* "What do you think is interesting about this? What do you like about it?" As Jason probes further, he asks the student to look closely at her chosen object and think of how it is used. Then he asks how her sculpture might be like the toy she has chosen. To a student combining a funnel and shell, Jason asks, "What do you like about the shell?"
- *Assess as you work.* "How is that coming?" After the student nods that it's OK, Jason talks with her about what she might do next. "What are you doing now?" The student and Jason talk about what she might do next because her sculpture is too wet to work on any more today.

Jason Reflects

In an interview after this class, Jason said he hopes the students will begin to internalize the questions he poses and get better and better at the habit of Question and Explain. He explained that posing questions helps students become aware of the choices they make as they work, a process he described as follows: "They have to identify the choices they've made during the process and experiment as well, and just be able to reflect on the process or reflect on what they've made afterward." He added that "when students say, 'Well, this is the way I like it. This is the way I want it.' I say, 'Why do you want it that way?'"

TEACHING STUDENTS TO EVALUATE

Certainly more so than in non-arts classrooms, students in visual arts classes receive continual training in evaluating their own work and working process, as well as the work of others. Art teachers frequently evaluate student work informally as they move around the room while students are working, and they also evaluate more formally during Critique sessions and when reviewing portfolios of students' work. Students can learn from these consultations and critiques how to evaluate themselves and others. Thus, students in visual arts classes are learning to make aesthetic judgments and to defend them, and because they are engaged in continuous self-assessment, they have the opportunity to learn to be self-critical and to think about how they could improve.

Sometimes teachers make quite specific comments about a student's creations, referring to particular qualities that need work, for example, and suggesting how the student might improve the work. At other times teachers make global comments about a student's work, such as "this is working well" or "this needs more work." Global evaluative comments that were not about a work, such as "You are doing a great job in this class," are not seen as Evaluate but rather as Engage and Persist; we viewed them as a way of helping the student gain confidence and thereby work harder.

When teachers evaluate, they are typically evaluating something specific, whether the technique, the expression, or the observational skill revealed. Thus, when a comment aims to teach the student to Evaluate, it usually is also teaching another habit as well. For example, if a teacher evaluates a student's technique, this is a way to help the student not only learn to *Evaluate* but also to learn *Craft*. Most often, Evaluate is combined with teaching Observe, because as teachers evaluate, they draw students' attention to specific aspects of the work, and hence hone students' observational skills.

Students learn to value criticism because they see that criticism helps them grow. As a senior at the Boston Arts Academy told us, "When I was younger, I wanted to hear people tell me, 'Oh you're doing so good. That's so beautiful.' And now I just want to grow. So by just hearing the good things, you don't grow" (see Figure 10.2). A freshman shows us that already in his first year at Walnut Hill, he has become able to evaluate his own work critically. Looking at some work done early in the year, he tells us,

> I don't think these are particularly well drawn. Because when I did it . . . I'd draw the head and finish it and then move on down the neck and into the arm. Draw everything piece by piece instead of drawing the whole figure which is what I gradually learned to do (see Figure 10.3).

Near the beginning of the school year at the Boston Arts Academy, the new 9th-grade students in Kathleen Marsh's class have been working on a series of four self-portraits in colored pencil (see also Example 5.2). Kathleen begins today's class with a critique followed by a Students-at-Work session (see Figure 10.4). We briefly describe the critique and several Students-at-Work interactions to show examples of comments likely to help students learn to Evaluate.

Figure 10.3. Late in the 9th Grade, a Student at Walnut Hill Reflects on How He Used to Draw Figures "Piece by Piece Instead of Drawing the Whole Figure"

DRAWING VALUES IN COLOR: SELF-PORTRAIT IN COLORED PENCIL PROJECT (EXAMPLE 10.3)

Kathleen asks students to put up their partially completed drawings for all to see. Then she asks students, one at a time, to select a peer's drawing and describe it using some of the vocabulary terms listed on the board. Students were then encouraged to Evaluate the work in process by thinking about choices they had made and Envisioning changes that they could make to their own drawings. Kathleen said that she placed the Critique at the start of class so that she could redefine the goals of the self-portrait assignment through this low-stakes evaluation. She wanted students to focus their attention on value and composition. To support this shift in focus, she highlighted student work that showed good use of value, and she asked students to think

Figure 10.2. A Senior at the Boston Arts Academy Describes How This Reclining Pastel Figure Shows That He Has Learned to Learn from Critique

Figure 10.4. Reflect: Evaluate—Kathleen Marsh's 9th-Graders Follow a Critique with a Students-at-Work Session

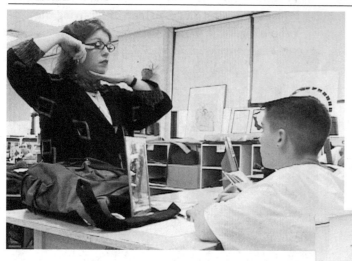

A. Kathleen Marsh shows proportions of a human face by using her own face as an example

B. Kathleen guides a student to evaluate his own work

C. Kathleen talks with a student about how his drawing can control where a viewer looks

D. Kathleen explains how she is evaluating a student's drawing

more about background (to develop Express) and the placement of the face on the page (to Develop Craft in the techniques of composition).

Critique

Kathleen initiates the Critique with a reminder to use this chance to practice vocabulary to articulate positive evaluations of each other's draft work:

> I'd like a few people to pick out the vocabulary words—and here they are listed on the board—that you see evident in your classmates' drawings. . . . You guys have really done an excellent job. And I'd like you to describe what it is that is excellent about these pictures. Pick one image and describe what you think is skilled or excellent about it, and use some of the vocabulary words in describing it.

A student begins, "OK, I like the outline there and . . ." When the student hesitates, Kathleen asks, "Can you walk up and point to it?" With this prompting the student points to a drawing and explains more: "Because it has a lot of *value*. Because on the right side it goes from dark to light and you can see different colors on the dark side. And on the light you can see just light. Like a little yellow and that's probably it."

Kathleen reinforces the student and turns to the student whose drawing is being discussed for self-evaluation. "I'd like to hear what you have to say about this. Apparently what you're doing is you're building up layers of color." The student responds. "Yeah, but I only did it on one side. I was going to get started on the second one." In what follows, Kathleen prompts the student to evaluate possible next steps in using color and value.

Kathleen: OK. So what else are you going to do today? What are your other plans for this piece?

Student: I'm going to make it look like real flesh, like flesh color.

Kathleen: OK, and . . . [*She waits for him to finish her sentence.*]

Student: And I'm going to leave it that light on one side.

Kathleen: OK, and what are some of the other colors that you're planning to use to create your skin tone?

Student: I was using like the yellow and light brown and peach and pink. I'm trying to get it to look like real flesh.

Kathleen: OK, can I make three suggestions?

Student: Uh huh.

Kathleen: Yellow, red, and a tiny bit of blue.

Student: Blue?

Kathleen: Yeah.

Student: OK.

Kathleen: Why would I say blue?

Student: Because it's a cool color. You want to mix two warm colors and a cool color.

Kathleen: It's a cool color. Blue is the color of your veins [*pointing to the veins in her face*]. And there is some of that in the transparency of your skin. A tiny bit. And also what makes brown? And I actually said this to a bunch of you on Monday. What are the colors that make brown?

Student: Red, yellow . . .

[*Kathleen calls on another student.*]

Student: Red, yellow, and blue.

Kathleen: Red, yellow, and blue. All the primaries make brown.

Having evaluated the need for mixing primaries to achieve flesh tones, Kathleen sets upon demonstrating the need to create different colors of brown because of the variety of flesh tones. Kathleen has all the students extend an arm into the middle of the table and observe their skin.

Students then move to discussing color in another student's work. When a student points to a self-portrait that he really likes, Kathleen probes for more explanation of that judgment. "OK, what is it about this that you really like?"

Student 1: Opposite. It's like the whole different contrast of the white and the brown is just there, you know.

Student 2 [the student whose work is being discussed]: It works out smoothly.

Kathleen: OK, but are you finished? How much white do you plan on leaving in your drawing?

Student 2: Umm, not much. Only the eye and some of the light . . . are coming from the other side. Like where the white is now is where the light source is coming from, but it's not done.

Often evaluation requires metaphorical thinking, as shown by the next student to speak who says, "I don't think he finished it, but I still think it looks really cool. It's all . . . it looks like you're standing there and all of a sudden a big flash of light comes and just brightens everything." Kathleen responds that this is a good perception and another student adds, "I thought of nuclear war."

A student teacher who has been with Kathleen all term joins the discussion.

Student Teacher: How many different colors did you use on the part that you actually finished?
Student 2: About like seven or eight.
Student Teacher: What were those colors?
Student 2: Yellow, purple, blue, brown like some brown orange, and a goldish color. Orange and a pink, like a pink. Or a mustard or something.
Student Teacher: So you use a lot of colors that you don't actually end up seeing as isolated colors within his face. But they all lead up to the illusion of the three-dimensionality of his face [*pointing to the portrait*].

Kathleen offers further information to enhance students' abilities to articulate their evaluative observations about the challenges of using the color wheel:

All of you guys are taking very different approaches to the use of color. [Student 2] has decided to make his colors really intense and keep that intensity throughout his drawing. And we've discussed how that might become problematic, because you're really working with that saturated color and you're going to continue to do that. Right? So I think you're figuring stuff out about color. Right? Because normally I would say start with thin layers and build up. But he's sort of layering as he goes. And that can be dangerous because you may run into problems that you aren't able to fix later. But you're figuring it out.

Students-at-Work

After the Critique, students work on their own portraits as Kathleen consults with individuals. To foster the habit of self-evaluation, her evaluative comments mix praise with advice for how a student might proceed:

- *Look at the subtle changes in skin color.* Kathleen praises a particular part of a student's drawing and draws the student's attention to a place where he has shown the subtle change of skin color when seen through glasses. "Nice

contrast in your skin between what's behind your glasses and what's on your actual skin. Remember we talked about that? How the glasses change the color of the skin behind them? You did a really nice job with that."
- *Decide if your composition is accurate.* Kathleen helps a student see that the viewer does not know where to focus because of his composition.

This still isn't touching any side of this page. You've got a floating head there. You need to at least connect this to the bottom and somehow figure out how to connect [the] drawing to [the] sides of the page. Why would I ask you to do that? . . . It makes that a bigger scale, but why is that important in terms of composition?

Kathleen points to parts of the drawing as she continues. "I am your viewer right now, so I am looking at your drawing and you want to be able to control where I look. . . . So your glasses really help and draw me into your face. But you need to figure out ways to lead me around your page."
- *Compare your drawing with your face.* Kathleen asks a student to see how his drawing does not capture the way her face is actually built. "My sense is the light is not hitting you exactly in half like that." As she talks, Kathleen gestures to her own face to demonstrate relationships.

Look at yourself. Generally speaking, your earlobes meet the bottom of your nose. So I think your ears need to be maybe a little bigger . . . and that will inform where the bottom of your nose is. And that will tell you where your lips will be. . . . Also look at the line of your lips. It's much curvier than what you have here, OK? Close your lips and look in the mirror.

This comment from Kathleen also prompted the student to Observe.

Kathleen Reflects

Kathleen believes that her 9th-grade students are not yet ready for a full-blown critique.

I think it takes time to work up to that point. . . . So we're not there yet in the 9th grade. Just to get everyone [to] talk in an orderly fashion and listen to each other talk. That's where we are. We're not there yet, the full-blown critique yet.

Kathleen used to consider effort as part of the grade, but she now believes that grading for effort does not show students where they need to improve. "It's not fair to them, because it's not giving them a really clear picture of what specifically they need to be working on." So Critique helps students learn about the qualities of work that matter. They are a kind of formative assessment.

Critiques also provide students with the vocabulary they need to talk about their work. She described many of her students as "intuitive art-makers." "They do what they feel without much vocabulary attached to it. So we give them this vocabulary that begins to really describe what they're doing." This helps students set clearer goals and also provides a basis for conversations between teacher and student.

Kathleen said that reflecting on one's portfolio and exhibiting work are two other ways students learn the habit of Evaluating. By keeping a portfolio and reflecting on it, students can see and articulate how they've grown, both of which help structure a student's thinking. She believes that exhibiting one's work is like a formal extension of an informal class critique.

Assessment happens on many, many levels, and of course in the older grades, I really believe that exhibition is a really key assessment tool, because I think in the act of sharing a work, and showing your work, you begin to—it's like releasing your baby. Once you release it, then it really becomes a separate entity. And that's when I think we really begin to look at the work and begin to grow.

When students graduate from the Boston Arts Academy, they must exhibit their work formally and talk about their work to a panel of outside experts. They must talk about their goals, their working process, their strengths, and their weaknesses, and they must answer questions. Students reported the value of this, saying, for example, "My perspective changed after my review because I was treated not as a child artist, but more as a young adult with artistic abilities." In short, when students are asked to reflect about themselves, they see themselves being taken seriously; they see their own interpretations valued and thus they gain confidence in their abilities to think about themselves as artists.

ELEVEN

Learning to Stretch and Explore

BEYOND THE FAMILIAR

I hope to teach the kids how to think differently.
—Mickey Telemaque

You ask kids to play, and then in one-on-one conversation you name what they've stumbled on.
—Beth Balliro

In the visual arts studio, students are asked, implicitly and explicitly, to try new things and thereby extend beyond what they have done before—to explore and take risks, to be creative. When teachers encourage students to *Stretch and Explore*, they do not tell students exactly what to do. Instead, through the level of challenge in the tasks teachers set for students and through the responses teachers make as students work on those tasks, they urge students to experiment, to discover what happens, to play around, and to try out alternatives. "See what would happen if . . ." "How else could you have done this?" "Don't worry about mistakes, just be brave . . ." These were all refrains that were meant to teach students to Stretch and Explore. Students learned that mistakes are opportunities—they can lead to new directions, and they can be diagnostic sources from which to learn.

In what follows, we describe two ceramic sculpture classes that show how students are taught to Stretch and Explore. Both teachers encourage students to reach beyond what they can already do and to play with alternative directions and possibilities.

INTRODUCING THE MEDIUM:
SKETCHING IN CLAY   (EXAMPLE 11.1)

At the Boston Arts Academy, Beth Balliro begins her ceramic sculpture unit for 9th-graders in the first class of the semester by having students "sketch in clay." Many of the students have never touched clay before. Now they must play a "game" in which they mold creatures out of clay and then destroy them. The end product is not important; only the process matters. The goal of the first part of the class is to get students used to digging their hands into clay. By working quickly and then smashing what they have made, students lose their inhibitions and learn to experiment—to sketch in clay—rather than create a perfect finished clay product. After the game, students work on a final creature that they will glaze and fire, so they experience quickly the entire process of wet clay to fired piece.

Students work in groups, sitting around small tables. A chunk of clay sits on each table, and Beth starts the game by telling one student to pick up some clay at his table and make "a creature that flies." After a minute, Beth stops him, holds up his creature, and says that he has made a creature that gives a sense of a creature that flies. Then she asks him to smash it. To the class she says, "The first thing I want you to get at is how to work quickly. The second thing, which is maybe even more fun, is destroying it."

Next, Beth asks one person at each table to pick up the clay and quickly make "a creature that slithers." After a few minutes, Beth tells each maker to smash what has been made and pass the clay to the next person, who will then make a "ferocious" creature. The process is repeated again when the next student at each table is asked to create a "gentle" creature. As they work, Beth moves from group to group, commenting on how each is doing. She tells them it is hard to just "dive in" to the clay and "smush things around." She adds, "Some of you guys might have trouble doing that. Especially some of you that like really clean lines and perhaps like to draw with pencils. Sometimes it's a really different thing to work with clay. So I want to commend you for all diving in. That's why we did that."

Students are learning to be messy and experimental—learning that this kind of mucking around is an important part of the artistic process. After the game, they each begin to work on their own imaginary creature that will be kept, fired, and glazed.

While Beth moves among students as they work, she finds ways to encourage them to keep working experimentally. "You might say, 'Here's a pencil, and I'm going to use the back of the pencil and roll it across the clay, and I'm going to experiment.'" The following are other examples of comments meant to help students learn to Stretch and Explore:

- *Don't worry about how the piece will end up.* Beth encourages a group of students to play freely without concern about how their pieces end up looking. She says that she wants them to have something in mind, "and then I want you to play and play and play."
- *Experiment with expression through texture.* Beth encourages a student to "think about what kind of texture it might be. Is it a furry part or is it sharp and shiny like a beetle?" She suggests that he can explore ways to create texture and should remember the finger marks another student used in her piece.
- *Experiment with tools.* Beth offers ideas of tools a student might use to experiment: "There's a couple of screws and things on the window sill over there and they make really good tools, sometimes, things that aren't really tools. You might play around with that, too."
- *Discover new techniques through play.* Later, Beth will teach specific techniques, but right now she wants students to discover techniques on their own, through play. Such experiences reinforce an understanding that techniques are solutions others have come up with for problems they have encountered. Students learn that when they have a problem, they can use techniques others have created, or can invent a technique to solve it themselves. To a student struggling to stick clay together, Beth says, "There are specific ways to do it, but I want you guys to play around in this first project. Just go with that and see what happens and maybe you'll learn a new technique with doing that."

Beth Reflects

Beth talked to us about this class and about teaching students the habit of Stretch and Explore. Taking risks is an important part of growing as an artist, which Beth says she is constantly trying to reinforce in her students. Her students "need to be able to risk what they're already good at" and not be trapped by the "safety net of style." Beth also talked about her own growth as an artist and the importance of stretching beyond her comfort zone.

> When I'm really working hard and doing good work, it's not fun at all. I hate it, and that's how I grow as an artist. I struggle through it, and I feel out of my comfort zone, and I'm exhausted, my arms hurt, and that means that I'm working hard, and that I'm growing as an artist.

One of Beth's articulated goals for the Sketching in Clay class was for students to lose their inhibitions about working with the medium of clay and about being "precious" regarding their work. She wanted students to free themselves of the goal of trying to make everything perfect and smooth. She had them smash their first pieces so they learned to let go, a strategy she has also tried with painting. When asked why she did not teach students about hollowing out their forms so they were not too thick to be fired, Beth told us that this was just one more constraint she wanted them at first to be free of.

As much as she can, Beth wants students to learn from the materials rather than through explicit instructions.

> If I had more time, I would have them learn entirely from the materials. And let them learn, and then fail, and then have things, you know, break and explode and all that, and then they'd learn that way.

Capitalizing on mistakes, she says, is a major consideration in ceramics:

> It's not all about perfection and dominating a natural material, but it's letting the natural material do what it will. So if something cracks, if somebody has a piece that cracks, I don't want them to freak out and think it's broken. If you have a crack, well, let's fill it with gold. And let's make that what the piece is about.

When students are playing, Beth believes they are more able to take suggestions and criticisms than when they are working on a piece that must be finished in final form. She told the story of a student who had a "white page issue" and how "it's easier for him to address it, deal with it in kind of a low-risk painting, which was a play painting, than in a highly refined major project." She added, "I think my hope is when they play around, stuff will come to the surface and then we can address issues in a less tense way." Beth also reflected more generally on how students at the Boston Arts Academy are not allowed to learn passively: "This is not just going to school. You can't just follow these rote things that other schools may have asked you to do. You have to really step outside your comfort zone and push yourself in all kinds of areas."

BUILDING FORM:
REPEATING UNITS PROJECT   (EXAMPLE 11.2)

For Jason Green's third ceramics project in the second semester of his mixed-age (grades 9–12) introductory ceramics course at Walnut Hill, students learn to plan in a responsive or "improvisational" way, by creating a unit and then repeating that unit to build a larger form. Students are learning to adopt the attitude of "what would happen if . . . ?" They cannot know what the end product will be like from the initial unit. They discover as they go.

In their first two projects, Jason's students learned traditional methods of hand-building—coil and slab. Today they learn a method of building based on repeating units, a method that is common in nature and often used in clay, as when walls of clay bricks or roofs of clay tiles are built. They are to create a unit and then repeat that unit over and over to build a larger form. He talks to them about different kinds of units and explains how the way that the units are put together determines the form of the resulting sculpture (see Figure 11.1).

Demonstration–Lecture

Jason encourages students to begin by playing around with different kinds of units. "I want you to experiment," he says. He discusses examples of forms from nature that are built up out of repeating units—a wasp's nest, a pine cone. He shows a small wall of bricks, and a sculpture comprised of stacks of the same cast bottle, layered over and over. The task for today's class is to create small experimental models trying out various units and exploring ways of joining these units into a whole.

Students are asked to decide how units will be joined. Jason tells them to consider whether they

are "going to be piled or stacked or are they going to be compressed together or glued together." Students are told to play with showing how the units are stuck together to reveal rather than conceal the building process. "You want to think about showing, if you stack things together, if you stack coils together, and assemble them; when you score, leave the connection and don't smooth things over." Jason refers to this kind of experimentation as "thinking with the clay." Here are some examples of how Jason helps students learn to Stretch and Explore as they think with the clay:

- *Experiment with a range of different forms.* Jason stops to talk with a group of students. When one tells him her plan, Jason tells her, "Rather than just starting, I want you to experiment with some different types of units. Some might be very geometric, some you might just grab and shape in your hand quickly." Jason suggests to another student in the group that she go even further and build using "dramatically different units."

- *Experiment with techniques for making and joining units.* Later, Jason returns to both students to talk further about different ways they could work with building from their units. To one, he suggests she might build something large by connecting together the pieces she has built already. Jason tells the other that he can tell her unit was made with the slab roller and suggests, "Think of touching the clay in a way you haven't touched it before. Is there a way you can make a unit just from your hand or from another tool that's not a ceramic tool?"

- *Think conditionally and experiment with what the clay can do.* Jason uses conditional, "what if" language to urge a student to think of possibilities for building a unit based on a wing. He asks, "What if you just tried flattening pieces of clay and building a wing out of this?" "What happens if you start alternating and building the sculpture up this way?" He also asks a student to make clay do unusual things: "Think about Jackson Pollack, because his painting was a result of his process. He would drip the paint in a certain way. How could you drip clay?"

- *Invent some different tools.* Jason tells a student to experiment with tools, including invented tools: "I want you to also do some more experimentation before the end of the day and make some things with your hands and with other tools that aren't ceramic tools."

Figure 11.1. Stretch and Explore—Jason Green Asks Students to Consider "What Would Happen If . . . ?" in His Unit Sculpture Assignment

A. A student consults with Jason Green about the units she has created from which to make a sculpture

B. Jason encourages a student to play with her idea of "wings" for her unit sculpture

C. Jason tells a student that he wants her to experiment

D. Jason demonstrates combining natural forms such as wasp's nests and pine cones

- *Take advantage of accidents and let things just happen.* "You are actually building a sculpture over there but didn't know it," Jason says as he points to a small pile of similar pieces of clay. He tells the student this is because they have a certain similarity and suggests maybe she try to see what she could build from them. He adds, "Those are interesting units because you weren't thinking about them too much when you made them."
- *Experiment with different versions.* Jason talks further with the student who originally based her unit on a wing and explains why he is urging her to think about several versions of the same idea.

> I want to put you through different ways to think of getting at the same idea. So if it seems like I don't like what you're doing, I like everything you do, I just want you to sometimes do different things so you can learn some more and see different ways of using the clay.

Jason explained to us that one of his goals for this class was to get students to explore ways to act on the material of clay: "I want them to research the material more than their idea of what their sculpture is going to be in the end, which is tough for them because I'm setting them down this road and they really have no idea what they're going to be making."

Jason and Students Reflect

Jason further explained why he wanted a particular student to think about the unit and not the final product: "The final product will emerge. Thinking about what the end result was going to be limits her." He added, "I'm really trying to get them to stretch and push the material and themselves, and take some risks and do some things that they might not normally do."

Jason also talked about his own habit of stretching and exploring as an artist: "That's what I do. I try to continue to ask questions, and because of that, my own processes are continually changing. I don't make the same things over and over and over again." A freshman at Walnut Hill said the same thing to us:

> If you know what you're good at and you just repeat that over and over again, you're never

going to get anywhere . . . you're just stuck doing the same thing over and over again because you know you can. And that's taking the easy way out. And you're not really going to go really far with that, I don't think.

A senior at Walnut Hill identified the habit of going beyond the given assignment as central to what she learned in high school: "I think the most important thing I've learned is thinking outside the box. Coming up with interesting solutions to interesting problems." She told us about how, in response to a multimedia assignment in her junior year that asked her to make a book, she explored different ways of conceiving of books. "I didn't want to make just any old regular book, so I started thinking of different structures that kind of had pages or had covers." She ended up creating an Asian-inspired fan with the different segments representing pages of a book (see Figure 11.2).

Stretching and Exploring is at the heart of the creative process. It is of the essence in open-ended activities with no clear right and wrong answers. Teachers of all subject areas typically hope their students will learn to think not only critically, but creatively. But it is in the art studio where creativity is stressed most explicitly. We believe that the emphasis on mucking around, trying out new things, and embracing mistakes as opportunities and for diagnosis are ways that art teachers foster creativity. Whether this stance in the art studio generalizes to academic classrooms, or even to life outside of school, is a question worthy of investigation.

Figure 11.2. A Junior at Walnut Hill Pushed the Form of Her "Book"

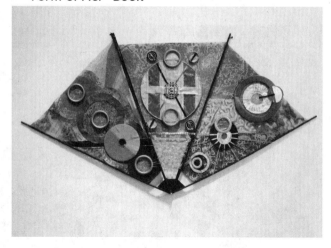

TWELVE

Learning to Understand the Artist's Worlds

NAVIGATING DOMAIN AND FIELD

Part of my role is to demystify art throughout the year.

—Jim Woodside

The most powerful experiences in art history that I have witnessed have been in my studio classes, not necessarily in my art history classes.

—Beth Balliro

There's strength in ideas . . . and working together toward a common goal.

—Kathleen Marsh

Relevance is a word often used in educational circles. What students study must be relevant to their lives—otherwise they will not become engaged. One way to make visual arts learning relevant is to connect what is being learned to its artistic contexts throughout art history and contemporary practice. Students need to see how what they learn in school connects to what people do outside of school. Just as students in mathematics class need to see the relevance of math in daily life and to understand how math is used in the real world, so also do students in the visual arts studio need to connect what they learn in art class to what practicing artists do, and to what the art world is like, now and in the past.

Students in the visual arts classes we studied learn about art history, the practicing art world today, and their own relationship to today's art world. They also learn to see art-making as a social and communicative activity. We call all of this learning to *Understand the Art World*, and break this Studio Habit of Mind into two components, *Domain* and *Communities* (or *Field*).

TEACHING STUDENTS TO UNDERSTAND THE DOMAIN OF ART

Students are taught about the *domain* of art (works of art, both contemporary and historical). While art history is not taught in a systematic fashion in studio arts classes, teachers often ask students to look at works or reproductions of works of art that relate in some way to the project in which the students are engaged. Students are taught about their own relationship to the domain of art, considering the similarities between the problems explored in their own works and those explored by established artists.

Students often talked about how their own art-making grew from looking at how other artists had solved problems. One of Jason Green's students tried to imagine the process behind artists' work so she could connect it to her own work: "When I see the other sculptures, I imagine about them, their process—how did the artist make this? How did they work? I imagine about the process. When I think about that, I can get ideas."

We first present examples that teach about the domain of art (artworks) and help students see the relationship between their own works and those made by professional artists. In these examples, students come to see that they are working on visual problems similar to those that artists are dealing with now and/or have dealt with throughout the centuries. They also come to see how they can learn from and be inspired by these artists.

CONSIDERING REPRESENTATIONS: FIGURES IN EVOCATIVE SPACE PROJECT (EXAMPLE 12.1)

Recall Jim Woodside's drawing project, Figures in Evocative Space, described in Example 8.1, in which he sets up a "scene" with two models, far apart from each other, just "hanging out." He emphasizes that "these two people are elements in a play here, elements in a drama." He wants students to use drawing to express a dramatic relationship.

To illustrate his point, Jim provides models of artists expressing relationships evocatively in paintings by Edward Hopper and Richard Deibenkorn:

This is a very famous painting done by Edward Hopper called *Nighthawks,* done in 1942. OK, now, if you can see it, what's the sort of feeling you get from this, what's the emotional content? [Students suggest quiet, late, drowsy.] Quiet, late, drowsy, how is that implied? It's a very quiet painting, that's a really, a really perceptive remark. And I really like that you said that, 'cause what you're starting to do is describing it not just in paint terms. It's a very quiet painting, it's late at night, the figures are small in relation to the space, the way that they're relating to each other, they're all sort of, if you look closely there, I know this is just a little picture here, but if you look closely they're all sort of in their own worlds. . . . He thought very carefully about the relationship between the figures and how that was going to be implied.

This is by a painter called Richard Deibenkorn . . . and while this painting is not as emotional as the Hopper *Nighthawks* painting, it is very much about how figures relate in a larger space. You can see the artist working in his studio, and this is maybe the model. It's a very standard scene, a very ordinary scene. The figures themselves are not really individual, are they? They're just elements there, just sort of props in an overall drama.

Jim has shown the students the Hopper and Deibenkorn paintings to inform their thinking about the current drawing challenge he has posed to them. He explains, "So this is the kind of . . . thinking I think will be helpful if you need to have an image in mind as you begin something like this." During the Critique following the assignment, students discuss how they expressed emotions similar to those in the Deibenkorn and Hopper works.

Jim Reflects

After the class, Jim spoke with us about how the image helped the students appreciate the challenge of the assignment, how he hopes students will move beyond "academic" art to expressive art, and how such paintings can help students understand what he is getting at:

When they look at [the Hopper] they don't think . . . "look at the figures," they think . . . "it's a late mysterious night.". . . And there's figures in there and they don't seem to be talking to each other and they can all understand immediately, even though it's a very dated image, they can understand that idea of hanging out late at night.

DRAWING INSPIRATION FROM IMAGES: AFRICAN POTTERY PROJECT (EXAMPLE 12.2)

Students working on Beth Balliro's African Pottery project near the beginning of their second-term 9th-grade class at the Boston Arts Academy are making a textured clay surface inspired by the patterning in African pottery (see also Example 4.1). They begin by looking at ceramics from three areas of Africa. Beth explains that this will give them some context within which to consider what they are about to start making. She focuses students' attention on packets of images she has distributed that illustrate varieties of African pottery. She asks them to notice the patterning and select three designs that they like. To get the students to think more deeply about patterns, she also asks them to make sketches of the patterns they see around their house. The goal of the project in class today is to begin to make three coil vessels, each of which has elements from the pottery of the three regions of Africa that they have studied, both here and in their humanities class. The challenge is to make the form and the pattern match.

The students also learn about John Biggers, an African American artist who studied the art of various African cultures. Students look at his drawings, as well as at images of pottery from Africa. Beth explains that she has chosen Biggers because he's an artist whose work was inspired by African art, as theirs will be.

Beth Reflects

After the class, Beth explained to us that she wanted her students to learn to respect another culture's art as John Biggers did. She hopes that her students will be inspired by this and will go on to research the art of another culture on their own. She also hopes to get her students to understand that art can be functional and does not just need to hang on museum walls; again, Biggers exemplifies this understanding. "I want them to think about art in everyday life and how they can actually make things to use and have them be artful and share them with people."

DESIGN INSPIRED BY OBJECTS: CERAMIC SETS PROJECT   (EXAMPLE 12.3)

The final project of the term in Jason Green's beginning ceramics course at Walnut Hill is to make a ceramic set, a group of objects that work together, and that includes one pouring vessel, such as a tea set (see also Example 13.2). Before they begin, Jason shows them a wide variety of "sets" made by ceramicists, objects that he has brought to class for the students to study and touch. He holds up specific objects and talks about how they were made. He explains how a glaze was applied. He holds up a ewer and explains what it is. He holds up some jars, pointing out how they were crafted:

> Look at how these handles are made. These are pulled . . . to give this sort of elegant curve. This spout and this spout are made from slabs, flat pieces of clay, see, and they're joined right here [*pointing to the joint*]. You can look at these different types of lids and how they work. This is a special locking lid [*removing the lid from the pot and reinserting it*]. That's a nice handle [*pointing to the handle*], huh?

Jason also points out that some of the objects have designs stamped onto them. "These are put in with stamps [*motioning to impressed designs in the teapot*], so if you wanted to try stamping, we have pieces of, lots of pieces of scrap wood or pieces of plaster. You can use anything as a stamp." Jason points out how some of the pieces are made using techniques the students have already learned. "This is made using that wax resist like I showed you and just taking a very small brush and putting the glaze where I want it."

As he holds a free-form pitcher, Jason compares it with Jackson Pollack and abstract expressionism: "This is abstract expressionist, using the clay very quickly, then using lots of slips, very quickly dripping slips." Jason holds up another object, explain-

ing that it was a sculpture made on the wheel. "Just a sculpture with this hole as the aperture where light is supposed to shine through and then hit the table." And about another object by the same artist, "The bottom is added on and this is just an oval thing, but you can see how this easily could be some sort of pot." Jason is trying to stretch his students' conceptions of the possibilities of ceramics (also nurturing the disposition to Envision). They have moved a far distance from ceramics as ash trays!

After studying the actual objects, students are directed to look at books and postcards and images on the computer (including images of ceramics from the Sung Dynasty in China) for further ideas. "I want you to think about just the different varieties of form and different approaches to touching the clay." Like the students in Beth's African Pottery class, Jason has his students draw their inspiration here from the art of a distant culture. Such exploration extends students' imaginations through connections to the ongoing conversation conducted in the world of practicing artists.

Jason Reflects

After class, Jason spoke to us about how he believed that looking at works by ceramicists can open up students' minds to new possibilities. He wanted them to see many options. He particularly wanted them to see subtle variations in form and to relate form to function. He believes that this kind of looking will encourage students to try new ways of working with clay:

> I brought in some historical stuff for them to look at . . . some of them have seen some historical ceramics. . . . It's just to show them these slight variations in forms and how they might relate to how the object is used. And just again in many ways trying to open up . . . their minds to all the different possibilities and variations that are available to them. . . . I want them to . . . be able to investigate . . . new ways of working and touching the clay. So I think it's good . . . for me to bring in examples that they can look at visually and also things that they can touch, and you know, learn as much as they can from that and observe as much as they can. . . . That's one thing I think I'm trying to also show them is there's such a huge variety of vocabulary available to them.

STRUCTURING A WHOLE CLASS TO FOCUS ON DOMAIN: CUBISM PROJECT   (EXAMPLE 12.4)

After presenting the examples above, we want to describe one class in depth to show how learning to understand the domain of the art world (or artworks) can become a thread through the three structures of Demonstration–Lecture, Students-at-Work, and Critique. For Jim Woodside's Cubism Project at Walnut Hill, students examine cubist paintings before and during their efforts to make a drawing in a cubist style.

Demonstration–Lecture to Present the Project

Late in the spring term of his year-long drawing course, Jim introduces students to cubism and has them make drawings based on what they have learned and seen. Jim shows a cubist painting by Picasso and explains that this is in the style of "analytical cubism." "It's the first kind of cubism," Jim says.

Literally invented by Braque and Picasso together. OK? They literally made it up around the first decade of the twentieth century—1907, 1906, around that time period. Now I'm going to give you a really quick lesson on this, and then we're going to start and you're going to do your own cubist drawings.

Jim holds up a reproduction of a painting by Delacroix to show the contrast case—a painting that is *not* cubist. What differentiates it from a cubist painting, Jim explains, is that it has depth. The surface is two-dimensional, but the artist created an illusion of the third dimension. For the cubists, the illusion of depth was "a lie" and so they rejected it. Instead, they wanted to show what was real. "What's real is this piece of paper, the flatness of it. So in a way, they were sick of lying. Now that's an exaggeration. Don't ever tell anybody that that's why cubism started because they were sick of lying. But there's a little bit of truth to it."

Jim goes on to explain how cubism differed from perspective drawing:

All art at that point, around say the turn of the century, the nineteenth to the twentieth century, all art was about depth, perspective. . . . You're looking into it. You're looking into a picture. . . . Cubists come along and here they're looking at

their canvas. Here's their big white canvas [*holding up large piece of paper*], and it's flat. It's flat. Two dimensions. One, two. How can we draw a picture of the world and somehow honor this flatness? Make that part of the idea? Make that part of the directness, the honestness of it. . . . They come up with this idea which ends up being called analytical cubism.

Jim follows this explanation with an example:

And what they thought was that if I'm going to draw [student's name] sitting there and I want to do it on a flat surface, I'm going to somehow acknowledge all sides of her. The front, the side, the back, and I'm going to put it all on the same piece of paper. So in a way, I'm taking the three-dimensional world and I'm putting it on a two-dimensional surface in a way that makes sense, that's logical and that's honest . . . it's important to understand why it ended up looking like this. It's not just a style. There was a reason behind it.

As he holds up several reproductions of cubist paintings, Jim asks students to talk about how each one "denies depth." He points out how one of the paintings violates perspective:

You know how I taught you in two-point perspective that as things go away, they get closer together? Look at this. This artist makes them get wider right there. That's not by accident. Why is the artist doing that? To make it flat. Why would they want to make it flat? Because the paper's flat and that's more honest. That's more logical. That's more contemporary, any of those words. But that's more real. Do you understand the idea? It's pretty deep stuff. It's pretty heavy stuff.

Jim then shows students Picasso's revolutionary cubist painting, *Les Demoiselles d'Avignon*, and offers an explanation. "Picasso is trying to imply all sides of the figure, the front and the back at the same time." He shows them a few more cubist works:

These are what early analytical cubism looked like. What does the word *analytical* imply when you hear it? Analyze. It sounds pretty dry, doesn't it? It sounds pretty boring. It sounds pretty, like, analytical. And they wanted it to be that way. Think about it. Think what I'm saying.

They wanted to honor the flatness of the surface. It's about analysis, like a doctor almost. It's not about wild expression. It's about how we can make it more clear, analytical, logical, honest. They didn't even want to use a lot of color here. . . . Maybe I'm making too much of the word *honest*, but it's not trying to trick anybody. It's not trying to show you a picture that doesn't exist.

Students-at-Work

Jim immediately moves students into their own drawing. "Think about trying to draw in that style today. Think about trying to draw the front and the back of somebody's head at the same time." He engineers this by placing a model in front of the class for 10 minutes, then rotating the model a quarter turn each 10 minutes that follow. Students must continue with the same drawing. As Jim explains, "You're going to be forced to draw several sides of him on the same drawing."

As students draw, Jim circles the room speaking with individuals about their work. He often reminds students about the core idea of cubism. When he spoke with one student, he said, "What you end up with is something that generally looks pretty flat. You know, meaning that you don't really look into deep space. And you know, as I said, the paper's flat. That's what those guys liked." He tries to connect what a student is doing to cubism: "They were inventing a new way to make art based on the materials. The flat paper. . . . So you already know how to do this. . . . It's just you're feeling, like, how can I draw like Picasso? If you need answers to this stuff, try to think about the Picassos." He is teaching his students that paintings by master artists can provide them with answers to problems that they are trying to solve in their own work (see Figure 12.1).

Demonstration–Lecture

Before the Critique session, Jim uses a short Demonstration–Lecture to reinforce the challenges and solutions of cubism. He brings out another cubist painting to show the similarities between this painting and the students' work. He directs students to look at the mouth. "It's a profile of a mouth, isn't it? And yet the lips are in front. So he shows you side and front in this almost ridiculous cartoon-like way. . . . That's what we're doing." He also underscores how what the students had done today is a continuation of the same things they had previously worked on in large drawings last week.

Jim stresses why cubism is something to internalize, to understand:

It's a really important part of the way art is taught, the art of the last hundred years. . . . Cubism is a part . . . of what you should understand about art, about Western art, twentieth-century art. And it's a very big part of the way that we work, the way that we study. And cubism itself is just a style, but that idea of the flatness is what I want you to remember.

Again Jim relates cubism to other things his students have studied:

If you need a simple way to think of it, think of it as the opposite of perspective. . . . I showed you before, months ago, weeks ago . . . about two-point perspective [*drawing*]. And how a railroad track goes way back in space. . . . And this is your canvas [*drawing*]. And this is your railroad track going back in space. If you're doing a cubist painting of it, there's your railroad track [*drawing*]. Right. It's flat. It's right here. Now this is really a simple illustration, but I'm only saying it to you as a way of thinking about a kind of oppositeness of perspective. And why? Because remember, the canvas is two-dimensional. . . . Cubists thought that the image itself needed to be a reflection of the two-dimensional canvas.

Jim Reflects

When we spoke to Jim after class, he offered these reasons for wanting students to understand cubism. First, students should understand the logic behind the emergence of cubism:

Cubism . . . was the most important . . . new movement in painting. . . . Kids can get a handle on this. . . . I think that they can start to understand or be curious about underlying . . . concepts in other contemporary art. . . . There are fairly concrete things to grasp on to, in terms of understanding it. . . . It's important for them to understand that it's not just a new look, it's not a new style that came out, there's a reason behind it. There's logic to it that somebody was after.

Figure 12.1. Understand the Art World: Domain—Jim Woodside Asks Students to Draw in a Cubist Style

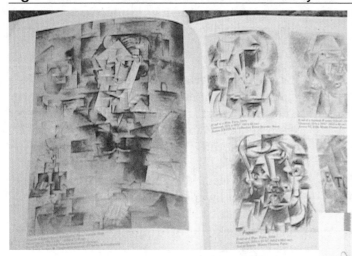

A. Jim Woodside shows students Picasso's drawings to support their learning to draw in cubist style

B. Jim wants students to develop a "casual relationship" to art in the past

C. Jim explains that cubism was motivated by wanting to depict the three-dimensional world honestly on a two-dimensional surface

D. Jim wants his students to understand that "art doesn't happen in a vacuum"

He went on to explain that students should learn to use works by professional artists on a regular basis:

> Students need to develop a kind of casual relationship to art in the past. To just go look at books, just flip through them, just get the stuff in their head. . . . It doesn't have to be this almost religious event. . . . You can flip through a book, and read a little bit here or there, browse around on the internet, and you . . . develop a relationship with it, just as you would with a person. . . . To develop a casual relationship is also to develop a living relationship. . . . The work has purpose for you beyond just historical significance. It's living, and interesting, and alive, and maybe you can imitate some of it [and make it] part of your work.

He also explained that students need to recognize that one can learn from art without copying.

> It's really important to understand the difference between the copying and learning from, and art doesn't happen in a vacuum, it's not all . . . magically generated from inspiration. [Art] happens from work, and it happens from knowledge, and it happens from seeing other works. In some cases imitating them, borrowing things . . . this is what artists of the past have done.

We asked Jim if he thought students should study art history in a separate course. He explained that he prefers his method—making connections to historical works of art when these works are relevant to what the student is working on at the time. He added, "I try to get them excited about it and draw connections. In my mind, that's more important at this age than an official art history class." Thus, the disposition to Understand the Art World is inextricably fused with *making*. Students, Jim believes, gain a deeper understanding of works from the past when they see a direct relationship between these works, brought right into the art studio, and their own efforts.

TEACHING STUDENTS TO UNDERSTAND THE ART COMMUNITY

Students are taught about the *communities* of people and institutions that shape the art world and how they, as autonomous developing artists, relate to its various components. Communities refer to what Csikszentmihalyi (1990) has called the "field" of art—the galleries and museums, and the people who guard and open these gates—museum curators, gallery owners, other artists (including peer students), and teachers. Together, these gate-keepers decide whose work will be exhibited and immortalized. Students are meant to learn about their own relationship to this broader art community. They think about how they might fit into the art community, what they might do after graduation, and what they have to do to get there. They learn how to present themselves as artists by matting and framing their work, making slides, creating a portfolio, hanging a show, and applying to art schools. All of these activities are ways in which students are learning to become professional artists. Of course, most students in art classes will not go on to become artists. But learning to understand the challenge of balancing tensions between autonomy and collaboration in creating works of art is important for both serious and casual students of art.

The community component of Understand the Art World also refers to how students learn to work with their peers. When they work on a group project, such as the creation of a library of ceramic molds (Example 12.6), or the Egg Drop Project (Example 12.7), they work in a team. When they work on individual projects, they share tools and materials, they help each other by providing suggestions, and they learn by looking at each other's work. In all of these ways, students come to see art-making as an activity that is not carried out in isolation, but rather one that is carried out in the company of, and with the help of, one's peers. As one Walnut Hill senior told us, "I think working like this [in the studio] with a lot of people and on my own made me be able to respect other people a lot more and have a better understanding of other people and who they are."

In this section we look at an example in which students are taught about the communities (or field) that shape the art world and their relationship to contemporary and historical artists and their practices. Finally we describe two classes in which students are learning about community as they collaborate on group projects.

EXHIBITION: MOUNTING THE SHOW (EXAMPLE 12.5)

Near the end of their last-semester course at the Boston Arts Academy, seniors are working on

Kathleen Marsh's Mounting the Show Project and preparing their pieces for an end-of-year exhibit in the school's gallery. They have each prepared a written "Artist's Statement" in which they articulate what they are trying to accomplish in their work. In the classroom, students are matting their pieces. Downstairs in the gallery, other students are spackling and painting the walls. Student curators in the gallery are planning how to hang the pieces. Kathleen moves back and forth from gallery to classroom. She speaks to the student curators, "You've already measured the gallery, right, curators? And you've designated how much space each person gets?" She then returns to the classroom, exhorting students to get their pieces chosen and matted. "I would say you have to put in a minimum of four pieces. . . . So as you mat work, you need to bring it down to the curatorial team."

Kathleen Reflects

Kathleen believes it is important for students to do the work of hanging the show themselves. For some students, this is training to be an artist. But for all of them, it's training to understand the end of the cycle in which they take their work out of the privacy of the studio and into the public, whomever their "public" may be. It's also a way to develop important skills—students learn how to curate, prepare and hang work, measure and fill space, paint walls, and consider the many dimensions of creating a show that works.

CREATING A LIBRARY OF MOLDS: COIL SCULPTURE PROJECT   (EXAMPLE 12.6)

For Jason Green's Coil Sculpture Project in the middle of the second semester of his year-long introductory ceramics course at Walnut Hill for a mixed-grade group of high school students, students create a library of molds to be shared later by all the students in the class as they make "skins" for their individual ceramic sculptures, an assignment that encourages students to share while at the same time pursuing their own work. Each student is going to make three different kinds of plaster molds. One will be a large slab with a texture all over the surface (the texture mold). Jason tells the students that "this is a very fast way to get a whole bunch of texture. So we're going to start building our sculpture using all different textured slabs. And we're going to share, OK?" Students will also make a sprig mold and a stamp mold. A sprig is a small mold that yields a

piece of clay that can be attached to the surface of a sculpture.

After all the students have made these molds, they will then begin to make a textured surface for their ceramic sculpture. Making this "skin" will be "a very additive process. You're going to keep adding to the surface. And it's going to be lots of different types of textures."

To make their ceramic "skin," students will be able to make use of parts of the textured slabs created by other students. "So we're all going to be making a lot of molds. And we're going to have a library of molds, so that you can have a sculpture made from all different types of textures." While students spend this class period working individually on their molds, they know that they are working to create a library of textures to be shared. As they work with the plaster molds, students also share batches of plaster.

Jason Reflects

Jason stressed the importance of collaboration when we spoke to him. He thinks it is important for students to see how others have solved a problem and for them to learn from that solution. Students can also learn by eavesdropping: When he works with students, Jason responds to the individual, but he is aware, too, that other students are listening.

FOCUSING ON STRENGTH AND FORM: THE EGG DROP PROJECT   (EXAMPLE 12.7)

It is not difficult to create collaborative projects in studio classes, and, indeed, visual artists such as muralists, filmmakers, or architects do create work collaboratively. However, such collaboration has not been the norm in the discipline of visual arts, particularly among graphic artists and sculptors. Perhaps this explains why we rarely saw team projects and more often saw teachers set up ways for students to support each other even though they were working autonomously.

Kathleen Marsh's class described here, the introduction to the final sculpture unit in the first term of the 9th-grade class at the Boston Arts Academy, is one of the few examples we saw of a team project. She divided the class into teams and gave each the same challenge—to create a container that will keep an egg from breaking when it is dropped from a banister down several flights of stairs. Each team is given one piece of foam core, three pieces of oak tag, ten straws, and a raw egg. They have an hour and a half to come up with a solution, to "create a safe haven for your egg," as she tells them. Students know there will be a prize for the winning team (or teams), and that winning means dropping the container and not breaking the egg. Another prize will go to the team that makes the best visual design. Thus, there is one prize for strength and one for aesthetics. Students must work together to solve this problem—there are no individual contenders (see Figure 12.2).

As students work, Kathleen moves around, directing comments to the groups as well as to individuals. In the interactions that follow, we see Kathleen focusing her students' attention on working together:

- *Look at a solution devised by another group.* "And can I just show you this?" Kathleen asks as she shows one group what another group of students has done to help them think of what they might do in their own work. "If you make strips out of your oak tag and fold them like this, you can make springs."
- *Remember you are not working alone on this project.* Kathleen continually reminds students that they are working together on the project. "Maybe two of you can do that while [she] is doing this?"
- *Keep in mind that resources are shared, and don't be selfish.* One group has used several eggs, leaving none for some teams. Kathleen expresses her displeasure: "You guys really put another team in a jam, and I'm not happy about that."

Kathleen Reflects

When we interviewed Kathleen, she explained why she believes collaboration and teamwork are important:

- Each student brings a different kind of skill to the group.
- Collaboration is a way to gather ideas and is also motivating because it is fun.
- When students work in a group, they keep each other in check so that the teacher does not have to play this role.
- Working in groups toward a common goal helps students transcend barriers of class and race.

- Collaboration is a skill that artists need, and many of her students hope to go on in the arts.

Although many visual artists still work individually, collaborative teams that use "ensemble" techniques, which historically were more central to methods in the performing arts, are increasingly common in the field of contemporary visual arts. Learning to work in and with artistic communities is valuable to art students for appreciating current practice. Working in communities also offers possible connections to the performing arts and to non-arts endeavors, such as science or interdisciplinary projects in which teams of disciplinarians from a range of domains work together toward shared ends. Again, though, whether the collaborative skills and attitudes learned in visual arts classes transfer to other learning contexts is a question worthy of empirical investigation.

As students learn about the artist's worlds, they connect what they do in school art classes with what actual artists do now and did in the past. They learn about art history by consulting the works of artists to help themselves solve visual problems. When working on portraits, they compare how various artists have depicted people in the past and the ways they are doing so today; when working on light, they consider the range of ways that artists have grappled with portraying light. Understanding art history is thus always connected to the student's own "making." Students also learn about the artistic community—the people and institutions of the art world sometimes called the field. This is part of teaching students to become professional artists, which is something many of the students we studied aspire to be. But even for students planning to study and work in other fields, learning how galleries and museums operate, learning to present their work professionally, and learning to respond to and critique the works of others are skills that help them connect their school artwork to the art world outside the school walls. And of course as students begin to work collaboratively (when art projects, for example murals or videos, call for team work), they come to see the act of making works of art as an ensemble activity.

In the next section of this book we consider how the Studio Habits of Mind are integrated with each of the three Studio Structures.

Figure 12.2. Understand the Art World: Communities—Kathleen Marsh's Students Work in Teams to Create Containers That Will Keep an Egg from Breaking When Dropped Four Stories

A. Kathleen Marsh offers suggestions to groups as she circles the room

B. Kathleen shows a group another possibility to consider in their design

C. Kathleen tells students to "create a safe haven for your egg"

D. Kathleen reminds students to work as a team

Part III

INTEGRATING STUDIO STRUCTURES WITH THE STUDIO HABITS OF MIND

Imagine walking into a studio classroom. Students are standing behind easels, using vine and compressed charcoal and black oil pastels on newsprint to draw a human model who sits hunched against a wall. Cool jazz plays softly, and bright lights cast shadows on and around the figure. The teacher is standing behind one student, silently observing him at work. After awhile, she speaks to him briefly, points to the model, and lays a piece of tracing paper over the drawing. She quickly redraws several lines, says a few more words, and moves along to other students. She continues her rounds, stopping, looking, talking, and modeling processes and possibilities in short conversations with individuals.

A knowledgeable observer might surmise that the lesson's focus is value—students seem meant to learn to represent the variations of light and shadow on the figure. The spotlights are set up deliberately to emphasize the natural shadows that fall from the figure's contours; charcoal and oil pastels, black, without the confusion of color, are media that readily convey variations in light and shadow. But as we listen in more closely to the conversations between the teacher and her students, we only sometimes hear her emphasizing this element of developing craft. Yes, she talks to her students about value, but she frequently mentions other elements of drawing—line, edge, composition. She also talks about the "feel" or "directness" of various marks and areas of a drawing, as well as accuracy in representation. She engages in a discussion about "how to take that further," and another discussion about the similarity of one student's approach to a particular contemporary artist, Philip Pearlstein.

She's talking about everything! In these brief personal conversations, teachers may focus on a single idea or process or Studio Habit of Mind, but, often, they address as many as five or six, or even all eight of the Studio Habits of Mind in a single, short consultation.

What's going on here? Is the teacher not focusing her instruction on what she really intends students to learn? Or perhaps this example shows that the Studio Habits of Mind are too narrow or too broad to be useful? Actually, we think all is well, both with the teacher and with the habits. The habits easily make explicit the quick and nuanced moves of an expert artist's thinking. An artist's mind flows dynamically from one way of addressing artistic problems to another, and the teacher's conversational shifts make that visible. Once a teacher makes her tacit expertise explicit, she can work on the elements of it that are of most interest, refining her teaching as she might her artwork.

So, perhaps the artist–teacher comments first on how she sees the work and the referent, focusing momentarily on the disposition to Observe. Next, she considers how she might depict the idea differently (Envision). Then, she may play with the idea a bit (Stretch and Explore), as a way to refine or create new techniques (Develop Craft). Without a pause, she might model different ways to approach the visual problem (Stretch and Explore), thinking aloud as she draws and describing what she sees (Reflect: Question and Explain; Observe), how well it works (Reflect: Evaluate), and how it "reads" to her (Express). All this can occur in under 3 minutes!

While the example above depicts the broad reach of habits as they are taught and learned in a Students-at-Work session, the Studio Habits of Mind were embedded throughout all three Studio Structures in the classes that we observed. Teachers addressed each of the habits of mind, individually and in many combinations or "clusters," not only in Students-at-Work sessions, but also in Demon-stration–Lectures and Critiques. The next three chapters illustrate examples of how teachers emphasize each individual Studio Habit of Mind and how they interweave the Studio Habits of Mind within all three of the structures by which studio instruction is organized.

THIRTEEN

Demonstration–Lecture and the Studio Habits of Mind

The Demonstration–Lecture structure is used to introduce ideas, assignments, and the particular Studio Habits of Mind that will be developed in the Students-at-Work and Critique structures to follow (see Chapter 4). As the teacher deliberately models working, seeing, and thinking as an artist, all the Studio Habits of Mind occur naturally. By slowing down the processes of making, perceiving, and reflecting about art and art-making for students in Demonstration–Lectures, teachers foster students' mindful attention to nuances that might otherwise pass by unnoticed.

FOSTERING PARTICULAR STUDIO HABITS OF MIND THROUGH DEMONSTRATION–LECTURES

In what follows, we illustrate how Demonstration–Lectures can promote the development of particular Studio Habits of Mind.

Develop Craft

Often, an assignment either requires or guides students to experiment with specific materials, tools, or procedures. Demonstration–Lectures, therefore, introduce students to particular features that are most likely to come up as opportunities and challenges as they work on Developing Craft.

For example, when Beth Balliro introduced clay to her 9th-grade students in her Sketching in Clay class, she showed them the practical realities of working with clay in their studio classroom at the Boston Arts Academy. She showed them where tools and materials were kept, what was available, when they could use them, how they needed to care for them, and even how to clean clay off tables and prewash their hands in a bucket so the sink would not clog with clay. Later in this same class, Beth assigned students the task of making a "chop," a traditional name-stamp used by potters. That provided further opportunities to clarify practical issues, such as the need to mark work for easy identification, to put work in progress and finished work on different shelves, and to treat unfired work delicately. She used the chop assignment as an opportunity to demonstrate the slab-roller, a large tool for flattening clay into slabs for a variety of handbuilding and sculptural projects. Such practical, grounded demonstrations greatly ease the inconveniences and minimize the dangers of working in the environments of studio classrooms, with messy materials and sharp tools. Through the demonstrations, students develop clear images of what they need to do and how they need to do it.

Engage and Persist

Watching a skilled craftsperson at work is mesmerizing, and teachers often use Demonstration–Lectures to interest students in the potential of techniques, materials, or tools that they can learn to use at high levels of expertise. For instance, when Jason threw spouts "off the hump" (i.e., he stuck a large mound of clay to the wheel, then centered and formed only a small chunk of the top, a technique that facilitates creating many small pieces quickly), the students' focus was palpable as they watched in silent amazement.

In addition to engaging students' interests, teachers use Demonstration–Lectures to model ways to Persist as they demonstrate some of the variety of techniques, tools, and materials that students might employ to address artistic challenges. For instance, Jason also demonstrated how to create spouts by "extruding" (i.e., using a wall-mounted metal pipe with a plunger, called an extruder, that can be fitted with different internal and external shapes, called dies, to make variously shaped tubes of clay), how to make spouts from slabs pressed in the slab-roller by wrapping them around cone-shaped wooden forms, and how to "pull" spouts off wooden dowels (i.e., a technique of repeatedly grasping and sliding a wet hand down a piece of clay to shape it). While no one student would use all of these techniques to create the pouring vessel required by the Ceramic Sets Project (see Examples 12.3 and 13.2 for a more complete description of this assignment), seeing such a broad range of possibilities encouraged persistence in finding and developing techniques that would serve students' particular creative intentions.

Envision

Demonstration–Lectures are a way for teachers to model a range of possibilities inherent in their assignments and help students open their imaginations to what could and might be done within the assignments' constraints. Recall Jason's spring Tile Project (see Examples 6.1 and 7.2), in which students were assigned to create low-relief sculptures of nine mold-pressed tiles. During the Demonstration–Lecture at the beginning of this class, Jason not only demonstrated techniques, but also showed students a wide range of images of tiles from different cultures. Kathleen did a similar "tour" of possibilities with a slide show of drawn self-portraits to introduce a self-portrait assignment to her seniors (in which students drew themselves wearing hats and vests they created themselves; see Example 14.4). By showing a wide range of examples that satisfy the challenges of an assignment in different ways, students are less likely to hold onto a mistaken belief that there is one "right" way to solve the problem.

In addition to helping students imagine possibilities for pattern, form, and color through multiple examples, teachers also help them envision the *process* of the assigned work. For example, Jason helped them envision making tiles by demonstrating step-by-step how to use tools and materials. He showed students how to build a mold box, how to press clay into it and how to get it out, how to arrange wooden shapes and other objects in the mold to create patterns, and how to consider common problems like direction of forms (e.g., letters come out backwards when they are pressed in this way).

Express

Teachers often gather a range of samples—of works, techniques, materials, tools, or ideas—to guide students' thinking about how to express personal meanings, feelings, or ideas in their work. Similar to the way Critiques let students see many possible solutions and hear many possible responses from their classmates, Demonstration–Lectures offer a chance to gain a wider view of the field of art, both from the present and the past. Such a broad and varied perspective encourages students to consider reasons for the variations that they observe, to think about what these variations "say," and what they themselves might "say" with a particular material, tool, or technique. For example, Jason often brought in artworks that he owned which were made by professionals (as well as a mud-wasp's nest that he had found in the clay studio and fired). Beth often copied packets of pictures for her students to achieve a similar objective. In Jim's opening class on contour drawing (see Example 15.1), he gathered descriptive words from the students onto a written list to describe the still life they'd been drawing.

> Just take a look at these words. Take a look at them and think about how this might relate to the way you're drawing. . . . What we do in drawing, we express things by the way that we put lines down, by the way that we draw. These objects don't mean anything. It's just some old junk I piled up here. OK? But, you're already making psychological, making emotional connections, making connections to other things by looking at this. We do this with everything. OK? So, [that's] what makes drawing interesting.

In Demonstration–Lectures, teachers point out characteristics of the works or processes of interest to students because of similarity to something they recently made (e.g., drawings of a still life, handles, spouts, glazes), or something they were about to use in a new assignment (e.g., expressive marks and lines, lips of a pouring vessel, coils, the mood or idea conveyed by a form or glaze, or the way a group of objects interrelates).

Observe

Demonstration–Lectures help students "see more" by exploiting their already developed interest in observation. Visual arts students are usually adept at learning from looking, and developing the disposition to do so is critical to their continued growth as thinking artists. For example, Mickey opens his 9th-grade design class session by introducing students to the Viewfinder Project (see Example 9.1). He asked students to use a viewfinder to "see the world in a new way" so that they could begin to stand back from what they *knew* and start to see the world as design.

Often, the processes involved in using and caring for materials and tools, and working with particular techniques, are complex, multistep operations. Showing these steps in the context of preparing to make something is an effective way of giving students a great deal of information in a sort of visual–temporal "outline" form, which they can then call back up when they need to refine their understanding. In an early drawing class on perspective, for example, Jim followed up on a Students-at-Work session (when students drew still lifes of boxes) and a Critique of those drawings (when students identified and discussed what "bugged" them about their work), with a quick, efficient demonstration of one- and two-point perspective drawing (see Example 9.2). By showing how to create a horizon line and a vanishing point or points, he could model how to draw boxes from any angle—a task they had just completed without that insight and which they would revisit immediately after the demonstration. Jim could then take the lesson one step further, by showing, through removing the rectangular case of an old film projector, how nongeometric objects could be "seen" through their geometry, so that objects of any shape could be understood through these simple perspective rules. His demonstration simplified to its essence a technique that can be very complex.

Reflect

Question and Explain. Because Demonstration–Lectures are generally brief, teachers do not usually dwell on developing students' disposition to Question and Explain work. However, the Question and Explain Studio Habit of Mind is sometimes fostered in Demonstration–Lectures. For example, as the teachers showed works of art, they often modeled the internal conversations that the creators of these works might have had while creating them. And as students become attuned to different features of particular types of work, they have a chance to practice raising questions and suggesting possible explanations for the forms, styles, appearances, or methods that they have noticed in their recent art-making efforts. For example, when examining a collection of vessels for the Ceramic Sets assignment (see Examples 12.3 and 13.2), Jason's students asked about techniques for making different vessel "feet," probably motivated by their efforts to trim the bottoms of vessels just before the Demonstration–Lec-

ture. They also focused on variations in handles and lips, which had been their recent concern in throwing cups, and on glazes, since they had just gotten their first glazed pieces out of the kiln. Both teachers' "thinking aloud" and students' practicing raising and answering questions help develop the Question and Explain disposition.

Evaluate. Similarly, Evaluation is a more peripheral focus in Demonstration–Lectures, but it is there. This Studio Habit of Mind shows up as teachers point out common challenges and solutions that arise from techniques, as when Jason pointed out how he was using his arm on his leg to build a solid foundation to support his throwing hands while working on the wheel (see Examples 5.4 and 14.1). He sets his own performance as a standard against which students can evaluate their own wheel-throwing. In addition, examining a wide spectrum of examples related to a particular assignment offers chances for appreciation of what works, what individuals like, and what is possible. All contribute to students' understanding of quality and help them develop their habits of evaluation.

Stretch and Explore

Just as the variety of forms, techniques, and materials that teachers use in Demonstration–Lectures allows students to envision more and to consider possibilities for expression, that range of possibilities also reinforces the habit of deliberately stretching beyond a current level of ability and responding to "errors" as opportunities—because that is what is modeled in the objects and processes the teacher shows. For example, in Jason's Repeating Units Project (see Example 11.2), his Demonstration–Lecture kept raising new possibilities for what might count as a unit (a bottle, a brick, a plug of clay, a cell in a wasp's nest), and kept raising "what if" questions about techniques (what if you ripped it with your fingers, cut it with a needle tool or with knotted string, or pressed it with burlap or the bottom of a cup). All of these possibilities helped set students up to explore, push beyond the known, and observe accidents as opportunities and options for creation.

Understand the Art World

Domain. Demonstration–Lectures are a prime opportunity for teachers to inform students about the context of the culture of art in which they are working as artists. Jim showed students historical works that drew on the processes he was asking them to try. Mickey encouraged browsing through numerous journals and magazines to find examples of design techniques students were exploring, such as fonts, layouts, and color schemes. Beth worked to expand students' attitudes about what counted as "art" by showing students the objects from African and Japanese cultures that they might otherwise see as "only utilitarian." Jason showed students books of tiles from contemporary and ancient Asian and Middle Eastern cultures. In each case, work by other artists (past and present) is used as a way to expand students' thinking about what is possible, what has been done, and what they might try. The learning of *domain* in the art studio occurs in the context of work that students are currently doing, and not as an isolated "style" that they should simply learn "because it's important in art history."

Communities. The teaching in studio classes of art history and contemporary artistic practice sometimes happens through Demonstration–Lectures that focus on grounding students' own work in the contexts of the work of others. When teachers model processes, focus attention on the work of professional artists, or show students characteristics of particular art materials, these methods all emphasize the ways in which artists have worked in their own historical context, which includes the relationships to other artists as well as the relationship to their audience. While we only rarely saw teachers introduce assignments that required students to work in teams (Kathleen's Egg Drop Project is a notable exception; see Example 12.7), we frequently saw teachers remind students in explicit and implicit ways in Demonstration–Lectures that they were artists, and that artists were individuals who worked within various communities.

These communities include the student–teacher pair, peers in a class, visual art students within a school of students, student artists within a local community of artists, and student artists operating within a community of past and contemporary artists whose works form a context for the students' work. For example, when the Boston Arts Academy seniors prepared for their senior show, Kathleen used a Demonstration–Lecture to focus on community by establishing a volunteer group to plan the invitations with a visiting designer. She also set up another group to decide how to allocate space equitably to feature each student's work. We also saw teachers set up assignments that required sharing tools or materials. Recall that Jason's students created a library of molds that they shared in creating textured "skins" for the Coil Sculpture Project (see Examples 4.2, 10.2, and 12.6).

INTEGRATING STUDIO HABITS OF MIND IN THE DEMONSTRATION–LECTURE

The next two examples show how a Demonstration–Lecture integrates several Studio Habits of Mind.

TEACHING THE THEORY AND PRACTICE OF COLOR: INVENTING COLORS PROJECT   (EXAMPLE 13.1)

In Beth Balliro's Inventing Colors Project (see Examples 5.1, 7.1, and 13.1), which is taught near the midpoint of her second-semester 9th-grade course at the Boston Arts Academy, she uses a 20-minute Demonstration–Lecture to introduce three purposes for the painting unit that students are about to undertake:

- Developing a theoretical appreciation for color (Understand the Art World: Domain)
- Understanding how to work (Develop Craft: Technique and Studio Practice)
- Helping students develop the disposition to experiment with materials and take risks in low-stakes "sketch" paintings (Stretch and Explore).

As Beth outlines the basics of color theory with the color wheel she has drawn on the board, the focus is on Understand the Art World: Domain. She asks students to copy the wheel into their notebooks and refers to it throughout her short Demonstration–Lecture, which now changes focus to emphasize Develop Craft: Technique. "This is a magical wheel, . . . because you can invent any color you want, if you understand how this wheel works." She explains that color is difficult to mix with acrylic paints, which they will be using (Develop Craft: Technique). When they begin to work, the focus will shift again to Stretch and Explore as students start to create a couple of "sketch" paintings. But, for now, the Demonstration–Lecture focuses on Develop Craft: Technique and Understand the Art World: Domain.

Beth uses the wheel to introduce primary colors. "You can't really make them. . . . If you were a cook, that's the first ingredients of your recipe, those colors." As is typical for Demonstration–Lectures, she introduces the information that students will use right away: "So the paints I'm going to have you use today. . . . Can you guess?" [*gesturing toward the board*]. The students respond: "Red, yellow, and blue. Plus white."

Next, Beth introduces secondary colors, again referring to the board so students see their relationship to the primaries—those colors mixed by combining the two primaries on either side (Understand the Art World: Domain). She suggests that the hue varies by the ratio of the primaries to each other in the mix and suggests that they experiment with that when they're working. "I want you to play today. You're really playing with mixing" (Stretch and Explore). Then she introduces the complementary colors, with reference to how they stand opposite the primaries on the color wheel and how they contrast with each other, and she closes with the neutrals: "A neutral color happens when you mix a color with its opposite" (Understand the Art World: Domain).

As the time to paint approaches, Beth sets the students up to paint experimentally by telling them that the color wheel doesn't work perfectly.

> *My* teacher said, "If you mix red plus blue, you'll get purple." So I took red, like the color of his shirt red [*pointing to a student's shirt*], and I took blue, sort of the color of his shirt blue, and what did I get? Brown. And I thought, "I thought you said . . . ?" What would be the problem there? Well, this red has a little bit of orange in it. So it's not completely true, but it's something to guide you. That's why I'm going to give you two shades of blue, because sometimes blue acts differently [*holding up two cans of blue paint*] (Stretch and Explore).

With the theory taken care of, Beth concludes the Demonstration–Lecture by showing students the materials they need to do the assignment, where to get them, and how to set them up (Develop Craft: Studio Practice). She shows students their palettes (new white Frisbees), paints (fresh tubes of acrylic), and new brushes, which she reminds them to use and clean carefully. She shows them how to set up their palettes with the colors in the order of the color wheel, shows them "gloss medium," to "make colors clearer" or "see-through," and shows them the paper they'll use. The students transition quickly to a Students-at-Work session in which they create two paintings of imaginary settings, one using complementary colors and one using neutral colors.

DESIGN INSPIRED BY OBJECTS: CERAMIC SETS PROJECT   (EXAMPLE 13.2)

The Demonstration–Lecture with which Jason introduces his Ceramic Set Project (see Examples 12.3 and 13.2), taught in the middle of the first semester of his year-long ceramics course, emphasizes the relationships among four goals:

- Looking carefully at objects to see how they were made (Observe).
- Planning ceramic design in a variety of ways (Envision).
- Making choices to convey ideas or feelings (Express).
- Synthesizing technical skills learned over the term (Develop Craft: Technique).

During this portion of his Demonstration–Lecture (which occupies 40 minutes), Jason shows students a range of tools, techniques, and processes that they might employ to express meaning in the design and creation of their "sets."

Goal 1: Observe

In this Demonstration–Lecture, Jason shows students several tools and techniques to add to their repertoire of choices for this final assignment of the first term. He shows them new tools (e.g., the clay extruder for pressing spouts, dowels for pulling spouts) and new techniques (e.g., throwing small cups off a hump that, when cut in half vertically, become pitcher spouts). He also shows them new uses for old tools and techniques if they are combined with new ones (e.g., using slabs to roll spouts around dowels).

> You saw the spouts over on those other teapots, which are made in a way very similar to this (Observe, Develop Craft: Technique). We can pull spouts on dowels [*beginning to form clay*]. Very similar to pulling handles (Observe, Develop Craft: Technique). You want to put this through the middle as close as you can get to the middle [*pushing dowel through the clay*] and you want to get water on this [*removing the clay and dampening the dowel*] so it slides and just like you're pulling a handle, you can pull a spout [*beginning to form the spout over the dowel*] (Observe, Develop Craft: Technique).

Goal 2: Envision

As Jason demonstrates the various tools and techniques, he emphasizes how students might think creatively about their use. The interplay between techniques and ideas, therefore, is modeled as seamless. He teaches his students how to make the leap between the concrete materials and tools and the aesthetic purposes to which they aspire.

You can pretty dramatically change the form of something by cutting in . . . and adjusting (Envision). Now all these connections I would score—slip and score—so they would stay together (Develop Craft: Technique) [*beginning to form and shape a spout and attaching the spout to the tube*]. But just to give you the idea, there's the spout (Envision). And ahh, something like this [*using the tube made in the extractor*], you could use [*beginning to cut the form*] and alter . . . in some way to make some weird spout (Develop Craft: Technique, Stretch and Explore, Envision).

Goal 3: Express

In his initial interview, Jason was skeptical about the importance of teaching expression. On probing, it became clear that he worried that art was often trivialized by emphasizing its therapeutic uses as a way of "merely expressing feelings." However, using our expanded definition of Express, which includes the expression of concepts, personal meanings, *and* feelings, we observed Jason including Expression as a goal in many classes that might appear on the surface to focus exclusively on skills. Jason shows that craft is necessary in order to express meaning.

As Jason begins to form the spout over the dowel (Observe, Develop Craft: Technique), he explains:

But as you pull, this will get tighter and tighter, so you have to keep adding water on this and making sure that it's loose and sliding. And then you may also put some sort of lines in [*forming lines in the clay*] (Express, Develop Craft: Technique). And you might do something like spin it [*spinning the clay, making a spiral shape*] (Stretch and Explore, Develop Craft: Technique). Then you can slide it off [*removing the clay from the dowel*]. Then if you really want to . . . give it some shape, you might have to turn it on its side and let that get leather-hard and then come back and cut it, the exact shape that you want it (Develop Craft: Technique, Express).

It may be difficult to understand why we label some of these examples as Express. Jason emphasized to us in interviews and to students in class that how artists touch clay leaves impressions that convey different meanings. A glaze applied with splashing "feels" more casual, so the object may feel more informal or convey a reference to the idea of

movement, as Zen ceramics often do. A smooth surface feels more worked, so the object may convey more formality. For these reasons, we see Jason's references to different ways to touch or mark the clay as emphasizing "Express."

Goal 4: Develop Craft: Technique

When Jason shows his students how to use a tool or technique, he almost always encourages them to think about the many possible ways they could use it in their own work. Thus, he uses a "cluster" of Observe–Express–Envision–Develop Craft: Technique to make sure that students are not only learning skills, but also understanding the artistic purpose and potential of artistic tools and techniques.

So, now we need to score this with our scoring tool before we put it together (Develop Craft: Technique). I'll score this side [*scoring the clay*] (Observe, Develop Craft: Technique). And we can press this together [*pressing the seam*] (Develop Craft: Technique). And I'm using this part of my hand [*pointing to the part of his hand he is using*] to try not to get too many fingerprints all over it (Observe, Express). And you might leave the seam (Express). If you don't want the seam to show (Express), you can also roll this [*rolling the tube on the table*] and later when it gets a bit harder you can come back with a rubber rib and go over that (Develop Craft: Technique).

With this ceramic sets assignment, Jason has helped his students develop a variety of Studio Habits of Mind. They learn to observe as they look carefully at ceramics; they learn to envision as they plan their designs; they learn to express as they think about conveying some kind of idea or feeling in their set; and all the while they are learning to acquire technical skills required for expertise in ceramics.

This chapter has illustrated the complexities and richness of Demonstration–Lectures and the role that they play in fostering Studio Habits of Mind. In the next chapter, we focus on the Students-at-Work structure, in which the assignments, concepts, processes, approaches, and attitudes introduced and modeled in Demonstration–Lectures are practiced by students as they create artworks under the personalized guidance of their artist–teachers.

FOURTEEN

Students-at-Work and the Studio Habits of Mind

Teachers may emphasize any or all of the Studio Habits of Mind during Students-at-Work sessions. Because Students-at-Work sessions always involve working with art materials, Develop Craft: Technique is a central goal. But as mentioned, this Studio Habit of Mind is rarely taught in isolation. In the individual consults with students, teachers often cluster instruction about a number of Studio Habits of Mind that help students understand the connections among habits and how to integrate them into their working process. Certain clusters of Studio Habits of Mind occur together frequently in a single student–teacher interaction. (For instance, Develop Craft: Technique was often layered with Observe, Envision, and Reflect: Question and Explain, and Evaluate).

STUDIOS HABITS OF MIND
ARE TAUGHT IN CLUSTERS

The two examples that follow show how teachers, depending on their goals, emphasize differing clusters of Studio Habits in their interactions with students during a given studio work session.

INTRODUCING THROWING: CENTERING
ON THE WHEEL PROJECT   (EXAMPLE 14.1)

This example is taken from a Vase Project introduced in mid-October in Jason Green's introductory year-long ceramics course for 9th–12th-graders at Walnut Hill. Looking at Jason's interactions with two students over the course of his centering lesson, we see how even the seemingly narrow technical issue of

trimming a pot can become a vehicle for students to develop the disposition to think with a wide range of Studio Habits of Mind. Two students, one advanced, one a beginner, are having technical problems with trimming. Jason asks questions that help them verbalize their technical difficulties and see what in their working process led to these difficulties. He patiently demonstrates techniques, observes the students, and guides their hands as they try techniques. He looks with them at other finished pieces to get ideas for successfully solving their own problems. When a beginning student is discouraged and wants to destroy the pieces she has built, Jason encourages her not to be too hasty in her evaluation, and to Stretch and Explore in her Envisioning of the possibilities:

> You should save a lot of your stuff even if you think it's not working right now, because since these vases are going to be put together out of different parts, you might be able to use a lot of the parts . . . even if it doesn't come out exactly the way you want it. It might not matter because you might cut it up and use it a whole new way.

Jason thus helps these students Engage and Persist through work they are finding very difficult. He frequently encourages them to keep trying and assures them that they will succeed. When the beginning student complains that she feels so far behind, Jason doesn't dismiss her concern, but responds in a reassuring way:

> Don't worry about that. Just [*laughing*] just don't worry about it, because your skills will catch up. You missed some classes so . . . most everyone in

here is two classes ahead of you, so they've had a lot more hours on the wheel. So it's easy to look around and see that everyone's making really tall things and you're not right now, but don't worry about it. It's still really early in the trimester so just keep practicing, and it'll come along OK.

When an advanced student feels frustrated with her lack of facility to achieve the delicate lip she envisions, he encourages her, saying she just needs to practice and showing her the precise skills necessary. He also makes sure to spend some time with her looking over her other work, pointing out its many strengths, and praising her on her progress so far, thus helping her Engage and Persist.

As these two students wrestle with trimming their vessels, Jason works with them to solve technical problems and thus Develop Craft. He also encourages them to look closely at their work and his demonstrations (Observe), consider their progress (Reflect: Question and Explain, and Evaluate), imagine new possibilities (Envision), move beyond their current capabilities (Stretch and Explore), and stick with it through difficulties (Engage and Persist).

CONNECTING WORLDS:
SECRET RITUAL VESSELS PROJECT   (EXAMPLE 14.2)

During her Secret Ritual Vessels Project in the middle of her second-semester course for 9th-graders at the Boston Arts Academy, Beth Balliro's interactions with students focus on yet another cluster of Studio Habits of Mind. An ongoing theme in her 9th-grade class is to build connections between students' art-making and their daily lives. Through a homework assignment for which she asks students to "spy" on how the people they know use various vessels in their daily lives, Beth inspires her students to notice the world around them and connect it to their learning in art. The day's lesson continues this focus on vessels, shifting to their ritual uses. Each student has been assigned a type of vessel to create secretly (an heirloom, something to hold holy water, a cat's water bowl), and they are to make a set of three vessels of this type. The aim of the "secret assignment" is to help students connect with the project (Engage and Persist), think about the function of the objects (Reflect: Question and Explain, and Evaluate), and create symbolic forms that the assigned function suggests (Envision, Express). Also, as is often the case in Beth's classes, her assignment ties into the school's humanities curriculum as she seeks to forge

links between students' own work and artworks produced throughout other times and cultures (see also Examples 4.1 and 12.2). This class builds on earlier field trips to the nearby Museum of Fine Arts. Beth often provides packets of articles, images, and information that explore artists, mythologies, or religious cultures. She wants her students to find links between their works and those of recognized artists.

Beth also wants her students to be able to articulate the thought behind their work—the process they went through in creating the work, the decisions they made, and the relationship of the work to values of subcultures that they understand (Reflect: Question and Explain, and Evaluate). It is not uncommon for students to spend part of the class thinking about a certain type of art, making written and/or drawn notes, and writing in their journals. Articulation is of particular importance to Beth in working with this urban population, and she sees it as a central skill to help these students gain recognition in the broader art world. In this class, the Students-at-Work session is followed by a critique, where students look at each other's vessels set out on tables for display, write their observations about each vessel, and guess the type of "secret assignment" for one vessel.

As the Students-at-Work session starts, Beth directs energy to getting students excited about the project. The prompt of their assigned secret vessel serves to get them interested and focused (Engage and Persist), and to find ways to adapt their own ideas to their assigned form (Express). As students consult with Beth about their ideas, they do a lot of whispering of their ideas to keep their assigned form "top secret."

Early on, Beth consults with students on their ideas (Express), on how to think about their assigned form by imagining and planning possibilities (Envision), and on how to connect it to the idea of ritual (Express, Stretch and Explore, Understand the Art World: Communities). For instance, one girl aims to make hers look like a family heirloom wine glass. Beth talks with her about the idea of making it look "old." For students who have a hard time coming up with ideas, Beth asks them questions or helps them consider what the key functional aspects would be. She encourages their thinking of different possible ways to realize the form (Envision) while keeping true to the constraints of the assignment. Beth also reiterates the key idea of functionality in her interactions. For instance, for a student who is to create a vessel that transports something, she suggests thinking about making a lid for it because that would make moving its contents easier. To a student making a very small vessel, she reminds her, "Remember this is for a human, not a mouse. It's so cute. But try to see if you can actually use it, 'cause I'd love for you to have something that you can actually use" (Envision).

As students move further along in the development of their form, Beth works with them to think about what they are making (Reflect: Question and Explain). She talks with them about the strengths and weaknesses of their pieces. For instance, she tells one student, "You've got a solid form and an amazing idea. What I would say now is deal with craftsmanship. Try to make it clean, perfect, beautiful, solid." She also challenges students to think about what their vessel will communicate to others (Express). For a student who is making a water bowl for a cat, Beth asks, "How do we know that this isn't to feed a big cat?" The student thinks and asks if she could write the word "bath" on it. Beth challenges her, "See if you can do it without words" (Stretch and Explore). With this assignment, and in each of these brief interactions, Beth reiterates the challenge to make an object's form express its use, a key artistic concept in ceramics. This project challenges students to move beyond their usual concepts of vessels and their uses (Stretch and Explore, Understand the Art World: Domain).

INDIVIDUALIZING DURING STUDENTS-AT-WORK SESSIONS

The examples from Jason and Beth show how teachers' goals for a given class or assignment permeate the casual, impromptu interactions during Students-at-Work sessions. However, another powerful aspect of the Students-at-Work structure is that it allows teachers to differentiate instruction without upsetting the general flow of work for the group. The two examples that follow show different ways in which teachers use the work session to individualize the curriculum.

DIFFERENTIATING FOR STUDENTS OF VARIOUS ABILITY/EXPERIENCE LEVELS: ABSTRACTION PROJECT (EXAMPLE 14.3)

It's the second semester in Jim Woodside's multiage drawing class at Walnut Hill. Some of the advanced students are taking this course for the second or even third year. All the students have had at least a full semester of drawing, experimenting with different types of materials and drawing from the figure and from still life. With this foundation, Jim's students are ready to move on to abstract drawing. Jim creates assignments that engage the wide range of abilities and experiences of his students and then adjusts his instruction to individual needs during the Students-at-Work sessions.

Today Jim has set up a massive tower of twisted paper stretching from ceiling to floor with lighting accentuating the abstract forms present in this still life. Students have positioned their easels around the structure, and, charcoal in hand, they prepare to draw. As they look at the still life and begin to set up their compositions, Jim tells the students to think in terms of dark and light shapes on the paper and says, "You can't look at it and get it wrong . . . so feel at ease." Over the next 3 hours, students draw multiple studies on newsprint. Ultimately, each chooses one of his or her sketches to develop into a larger finished drawing.

Over the course of this working session, Jim brings the class together several times for Critiques. He punctuates the Students-at-Work sessions with mini-Demonstration–Lectures about how to observe and draw shapes and the still life. Jim balances the need to develop less-experienced students' observational skills and techniques with challenging students with stronger backgrounds in drawing to enhance their more developed skills.

Jim has designed a project that will accommodate this wide range of learners. Considering their drawing experiences from the first semester and the technical skills they developed, he now wants to challenge students to explore the concept of abstraction—a concept that Jim recognizes may be difficult for his students. In an interview, he tells us:

Abstract art, to a lot of people, is sort of fringe and something that eccentrics and intellectuals talk about. I mean, these are stereotypes about, caricatures of it. And I'm not saying to them that I understand it all myself, you know. Or that I like it all. . . . But I want them to know that it really grows out of the same stuff that all art grows out of. And they can learn to evaluate it, and they can learn to understand it themselves. And the best way for them to do it is . . . to begin to do it themselves. And that's what I mean. And so . . . what I'm doing here is a little bit artificial and forced, setting up a way for that to happen for them.

The large still life in the center of the room is not an uncommon set-up in Jim's class. Observing a still life, choosing compositions from different points in the room, creating multiple sketches with various materials, and working toward a more finished piece over the course of several weeks are all familiar activities by this point in the year. Jim deliberately decided to design an assignment similar in scope and feel to the representational drawing with which students had become comfortable earlier in the semester. He wants students to see the link between representational and abstract drawing. Briefly explaining that abstraction is an important art world concept (students are well aware of this but hesitant nonetheless), Jim gently encourages students to do what they always do when looking at a still life. "Draw what you see," he tells them. By now this phrase is a familiar mantra in the class, so students can easily prepare for this otherwise novel task of observing and trying to make sense of the crumpled paper still life. Over the course of the afternoon, students begin to see connections to the drawings they made earlier in the year: They see that they are still working with shapes and lines and value.

Helping students build a bridge between representational drawing and abstraction is the primary goal of the class. However, Jim adjusts how he talks to students according to their individual needs. In what follows, Jim works with two beginning students, one who is struggling with the assignment, and one who has more confidence, excitement, and skills.

At five separate times throughout the working session, Jim consults with a 9th-grader new to the school who has limited English skills. About a half hour into the class, Jim notices that this student's page is sparse and that he looks confused. Jim takes the student aside and spreads another student's work out on the floor. He asks the student to observe the series of sketches and notice how each drawing is different. By looking at the work, the student could see how his peer deliberately changed the way she thought about each drawing, purposely using different lines and patterns each time. During this mini-Critique, Jim not only supports the beginning student in overcoming his initial obstacles with the assignment (Engage and Persist), but also helps him refine his observational habits (Observe). Most important, through the example of a peer's success, Jim encourages the student to move beyond his current abilities and try new ways of seeing the still life (Stretch and Explore). As Jim explains to us later:

I want him to throw himself into the act of drawing. Have fun with it. He really needs to loosen up and really put forms down and manipulate them on the page, and in a big bold way. So I'm always trying to get him to do that, because he doesn't. He's always watching himself. There are all the other kids in the room. And he doesn't have as much experience. . . . But what I was really doing there was showing him an example of a kid from the previous day who I would say is in a somewhat similar situation. And I think giving him a real clue to how to go about it. That helps artistically for him. And also language, you know, he needs to see something. So I was trying to explain that in as simple terms as I could, but I know he didn't understand the whole of it. So giving him an example I thought helped.

A little later, Jim briefly checks in with the student again and encourages him to use the viewfinder, a tool for designing compositions that Jim has frequently employed and discussed in earlier observational drawing sessions (see Examples 4.3, 5.3, and 9.2). Returning to him later, Jim watches the student working and notices that he is looking at too small an area of the paper still life and is not attending to the larger shapes that would help him make the bridge between observation and abstraction. He sits at the student's drawing easel and demonstrates looking too closely at the paper and how it keeps him from seeing the structural forms in the twisted paper. By explicitly demonstrating both technical drawing skills and the *process* of observing, Jim encourages the student to develop new habits of looking. By drawing on his sketch and then referring to the still life, Jim shows the student how to see the large shapes and learn to improve his own technical drawing skills (Observe, Reflect, Develop Craft: Technique).

It's now halfway through the class, and the beginning student has made some progress in identifying and drawing large shapes. In his next consult, Jim encourages him to go even further in pushing the lights and darks by using a kneaded eraser on his drawing, a new technique for the student (Stretch and Explore). Jim demonstrates this process right on the drawing, so the student can see clearly how to juxtapose a white surface with a dark black shading to make the forms on his page look like the crumpled paper he is trying to draw (Develop Craft: Technique, Observe).

In the last few minutes of the class, Jim compliments the student's work (Engage and Persist) and gives him some final bits of technical advice, demonstrating how to use white charcoal to make his contrast even stronger (Develop Craft: Technique, Stretch and Explore).

Jim works quite differently with a more confident beginner. With the first student, Jim needed to help him engage with the assignment, use visual techniques to work around the student's limited English proficiency, develop basic drawing techniques, and start to develop a way of observing the structure of the still life that would help him eventually bridge to ideas of abstraction. This next student, on the other hand, starts off excitedly, with a clear plan of what he wants to do. For his first study, he has darkened his whole page and is using an eraser to depict where the light falls on the paper. Jim supports this idea but also encourages him to explore more of the central ideas of the abstraction in this phase by doing multiple studies rather than focusing so much on technique:

> That's really good. That's a good idea, and it would be good for you, and I don't want to discourage that. But I also don't want in this drawing for you to get too much into refining that technique. I want you to think about how those shapes relate to the four sides of the paper. So on your next one, let your approach be a little more with that in mind (Stretch and Explore).

When Jim next returns to this student, he encourages him to explore abstraction further. He tells him to depart from drawing strictly what he observes and become more logical about what he puts on the paper. "I think you should proceed almost like it's a math problem. Like very logically." He shows him how he can develop a "system" for thinking about which lines should be dark and which should be light (Envision). He gives him some tools to do this. He tells him to develop a plan, such as making all the larger forms darker. When the student seems a bit hesitant ("Outline it?"), Jim explains a core idea of abstraction: "That way there's a purpose for what you're doing. It's not just decorating your drawing. And that logic is really important, especially in an abstract drawing. It gives you a sense of purpose and relationship to what you're doing" (Stretch and Explore, Understand the Art World: Domain).

After students have done several studies, Jim breaks up the working session with a Critique in which he discusses each student's work. When he discusses one student's work, he comments that it seems to be the one that has gone furthest to abstraction, where you no longer easily connect it to its original source of the still life. He uses the student's piece to reiterate a central idea of abstract drawing. "It's a texture on a piece of paper, and it's a way of organizing a piece of paper. That's what abstract art is. You're taking references from the world and you're organizing them into a two-dimensional world of your own." Following this group critique, the second student walks up to Jim and talks with him about his piece, saying that he's not really pleased with how the lines are working, mentioning his ideas for further work. Jim offers suggestions and supports the student's ideas. Jim reiterates the idea that the goal is to explore options, reminding him "this is just a learning process here" (Stretch and Explore).

INDIVIDUALIZING FOR MULTIPLE AGENDAS: CREATING HAT AND VEST PROJECT (EXAMPLE 14.4)

While Jim's example is about individualizing for a range of experience and ability levels, Kathleen Marsh's story in this Students-at-Work session, taught near the beginning of her second-semester class with seniors at the Boston Arts Academy, is one of a teacher multitasking to keep students on track with the assignment at hand and to help individual students with their outside work.

It's the first day of the final semester for Kathleen's 12th-graders. There's a lot going on, and Kathleen must prepare her students for the final push of their high school art careers. They are in the process of applying to colleges and art schools or preparing for jobs upon graduation. Not only do they need to have their professional portfolios in order, they also need to meet their graduation requirements, which include showing and defending their work in a senior exhibition. The students are somewhat distracted by all these outside events and battling a case of spring semester "senioritis."

Kathleen has much to accomplish in this class session. She introduces students to the current assignment of a self-portrait wearing a hat and vest that they have designed and created out of paper. She also introduces them to what they will be doing over the course of the semester, as well as going over what, as seniors, they will be doing outside of the class. She gives an introduction to the course requirements and reviews the syllabus. Kathleen discusses the defense process and her plans for curating the show and taking slides of finished work. Since students are putting together their final portfolios, she reminds them of this by introducing a several-week self-portrait assignment that will result in a finished value drawing that can be a "showcase piece" in their portfolios.

Today is the first installment of this self-portrait assignment. In this class, students create wearable paper hats and vests from oak tag that express something about their identity. In later sessions, they will make charcoal value drawings of themselves wearing the paper clothing. Today's portion of the assignment challenges students to both Envision and Express something about themselves, as they must imagine what the hats and vests they make now will convey about themselves, and how they will look as they wear them for their value drawings. As seniors, the students are accustomed to working independently. However, Kathleen monitors their progress on this assignment, including instructing and getting materials for students who are proceeding ahead of others to the next phase of the assignment.

While students create the hats and vests, Kathleen consults with each student about the progress of his or her portfolio and completion of tasks for the senior exhibition. This is in part an administrative task to make sure the students are on target in their application process, but it can also be a chance to model an important process of evaluation. For instance, Kathleen spends time with one student, looking over each piece of his portfolio, discussing ways of finishing some of the pieces, and identifying

which ones he should include in the senior show. She later explained that this is one of the strongest students in the class, but he had initially only selected two pieces to include in the show. Kathleen discussed working over the course of several years with this student on his tendency toward perfectionism and being overly self-critical.

The flexibility of the Students-at-Work session allows Kathleen to keep the group focused on their work, while also adapting to students' varying work paces on a multiphase assignment. In addition, she has many chances to address crucial issues with each student that are not tied explicitly to this class assignment. In a single working session, Kathleen is able to keep the class as a whole engaged in working (Engage and Persist), while connecting with individual students on issues central to their development as artists, such as the preparation of their portfolios (Reflect: Evaluate, Develop Craft: Studio Practice and Technique) and progress in applying to college and/or art school (Understand the Art World: Communities).

This chapter has illustrated how teachers use Students-at-Work sessions to keep their art-making goals at the center of the learning process while personalizing instruction to suit a range of student needs. The Studio Habits of Mind emphasized by an assignment sometimes take a back seat to habits of importance to a particular student at a given time. In the Critique structure, described in the chapter that follows, both general and personal goals become the focus.

FIFTEEN

Critique and the
Studio Habits of Mind

Critiques, by their very nature, foster the Studio Habit of Mind of Reflect: Question and Explain and, especially, Evaluate—learning how to judge what makes one work better or more effective than another. However, in the Critiques we observed, learning to evaluate works was only one of many goals. In every Critique we analyzed, teachers intended to teach at least five of the Studio Habits of Mind.

TEACHING STUDIO HABITS
OF MIND THROUGH CRITIQUE

Develop Craft

Looking at students' work collectively often provides illustrations of how particular techniques can function differently in different works, which can help students expand their ideas about craft. In addition, techniques are often offered as solutions to problems that students identify in works. For instance, in one of Jim Woodside's Critiques, he asked students to identify errors in perspective in their own work, and they worked together to figure out how to correct them.

Engage and Persist

Critiques can be highly motivating. Knowing that everyone is going to look at and comment on their work can spur students to put their full effort into it. In addition, the critique process can engage students by giving them new insights into their work. For instance, Jim often uses Critiques at the early stage of a drawing to help students identify the potential of a piece and to get them excited about its possibilities. Midprocess Critiques can also help students work through difficulties in a piece, either by identifying unrecognized strengths in their work, or by offering specific advice on aspects that they could change. In Critiques, the current piece is treated as an opportunity for deeper commitment to work and learn. For instance, Jason tells a student, "The glaze is transparent because you put it on thin. But you can try re-firing that and put the same glaze on thicker."

Envision

As students stand before their work, they are encouraged to think about what would have happened if they had done it another way. For instance, Kathleen Marsh asks a student to think about how much white space he intended to leave in his self-portrait. Jim Woodside asks students to imagine how one student's drawing would look if she had fully drawn the leg rather than leaving it unfinished. Mickey Telemaque asks students to think of ways a given photo could heighten its focus on light as the subject. Frequently in Critiques, teachers also specifically ask students to envision how they will finish a piece, or what they envision working on next.

Even without direction, as students look at and discuss each other's work, they envision different possibilities for how the work could look. In a senior Critique session, students' comments frequently involve envisioning their own and other students' pieces differently. For instance, one student notes, "It would just be a really nice photo if that wasn't there and there weren't arms just showing."

Express

Critiques offer an important chance for students to get some distance and recognize some of the global properties conveyed in their work that they might miss while immersed in the process of making. In addition, Critiques offer a chance for students to hear how others interpret their work. One of Mickey's design students described finding out that while her intention in a flag design was to celebrate her native Puerto Rico by showing that it was so "hot," other students interpreted it as an image of burning the Puerto Rican flag. Critiques offer a testing ground for finding out how one's work communicates.

Observe

The type of observation most particular to Critiques is that of observing works in comparison to one another. During the process of making works, most of the observation involves students looking carefully at their own work, and in the case of observational drawing, looking at the relationship between the work and the referent. In Critiques, the focus shifts. Generally, observing in Critiques involves looking at your own work in the context of pieces created by other students or in relation to multiple drawings of your own. Teachers often encourage specific observational comparisons, such as when Kathleen asked students to notice what different colors contributed to the skin tones in students' portraits or when Jim asked students to compare the expressive effects of different types of line quality.

Reflect

Question and Explain. More so than at any other time in the studio class, reflecting about student work is highlighted during Critiques. Teachers strive to draw students into a discussion that moves beyond just noting what they like and dislike, and into observing in the context of particular artistic concepts. Critiques are often framed around a set of targeted questions, such as when Mickey asked his photography students, "Why is this a photograph about light? All photographs depend on light; how are these [for the light assignment] different from every other photograph?" Another example is when Beth Balliro asked students to guess the intended function of their fellow students' clay vessels and to start thinking about the relationship between the vessels' form and their ritual functions.

Evaluate. Critiques offer an important chance for students to evaluate their own and peers' work. Critiques often begin with the teacher asking which of the drawings students think work and why, or asking them to comment on what works or doesn't work in their own piece. Sometimes an evaluative process precedes the Critique; students might be asked to choose their best work to put up for critique. Evaluation in Critiques is often analytical. Rather than merely sorting "good" from "bad" work, students learn to identify which aspects of a work are most effective and which may detract from the effect of a piece. As Jason explains, "I really try not to say something's good or bad. I just say this is what it is communicating."

Stretch and Explore

Just seeing the range of work produced by the group may push individual students to expand their thinking about their own work. To foster the Stretch and Explore aspect of Critique, teachers assign projects that are likely to yield diverse results. For example, Jason Green spoke about deliberately choosing glazes that produce widely varying results in order to promote more student exploration. During Critiques, he invited students to analyze the results of their explorations of materials much as they would analyze a scientific experiment. When errors are the focus, they serve as a chance to diagnose and/or as an opportunity for a work to grow in new directions. But the responses that students receive in a Critique generally do not emphasize failures. Rather, Critiques offer suggestions for how to think about what can be seen in the work and how the student artist might explore other possibilities.

Understand the Art World

Domain. Teachers draw connections between student art and professional art, and they make allusions to historical art references as they point out features in students' work. They may tell students that their work reminds them of a particular artist, sometimes showing them a print or two. This informs students about the larger culture of art and art history, but its greater purpose appears to be to emphasize students' connections to the historical and current community of working artists. For instance, during a Critique, Jim Woodside commented on one student's developing a certain "electric line quality" and use of space in his work:

He's really finding a way to draw, a kind of language that's his own, that will succeed for him as he approaches different kinds of problems. But that's something that he came up with really on his own, playing around with this project [*pointing to self-portrait from previous class*]. And I certainly think it's something that he can take into the way that he draws something like this [*holding up a sketch that the student is currently working on*]. . . . It reminds me of a Dubuffet painting.

In this Critique, Jim identified aspects of a student's emerging style and tied it to the larger art world.

Teachers present Critiques as reflective processes, including evaluation, that happen in professional arts communities, and not merely as isolated elements of an art class. As Beth prepares 9th-graders for a Critique, for example, she explains that Critiques are part of being an artist and that some Critiques are meant to be about evaluation, while others focus more on other aspects of reflection.

Communities. The social aspect of Critique is one of its defining features. Teachers focus on how students learn to value responses from peers and on ways to offer respectful and constructive criticism to their peers. Critiques reinforce the idea that art-making is a communal process, not only a private activity. Art is made to be shown to others and discussed, and that can be learned through the social process of Critique.

INTEGRATING STUDIO HABITS OF MIND THROUGH CRITIQUE

The eight Studio Habits of Mind fostered by Critiques are usually not discussed separately, but rather are integrated flexibly during Critique sessions. This integration is illustrated by the following examples of Critiques from Jim Woodside's drawing class at Walnut Hill.

COMPARING WORKS:
CONTOUR DRAWING PROJECT   (EXAMPLE 15.1)

While each teacher we observed held a Critique at least once, Jim held multiple Critiques in nearly every class session of his multiage drawing class. These Critiques were not necessarily formal, lengthy discussions; sometimes they lasted only a few minutes. However, Jim's consistent use of Critiques stresses the importance he places on coming together as a group to look at and discuss the work that has been done.

In the first class session of the year in Jim's drawing course, he introduces Critiques as a central but informal part of the routine:

What we'll do is, we'll draw for a while. Then we'll put some drawings up on the wall, and we'll start to look at them and talk about them. And that's something we'll do a lot in this class. Those of you that have had me before, we, we always do that—we draw, put the drawings up, talk about them.

After the students do a few quick drawings of the still life, some blind contour (in which students do not look at the paper but only at the referent) and some in which students look at both the still life and the drawing, Jim asks each student to hang a blind and nonblind drawing next to each other. Before beginning the discussion, Jim gives the students a specific thinking task to guide their observation and reflection: "Everybody take a look at their two drawings, and just think in your mind how to compare the two. Just to describe the difference between your two drawings." This task helps students integrate learning how to Observe with learning to Reflect. Jim encourages them to evaluate their works, asking which they preferred and why.

As students make comments, Jim acknowledges and expands on their responses in a positive and encouraging way. For instance, one student says of a blind drawing, "Notice all her details are not . . . it's detailed but it's not." Jim affirms her evaluation and draws this comment into its fuller meaning:

It's detailed but it's not. Yeah, that's really good. I couldn't have said it that well. That's very true. I mean, we have all the information here [*pointing to a section of the drawing*], we know it's there, yet it doesn't seem like it's overly precise, or overly worked.

In this first class session, he wants to ensure that students feel comfortable talking in the group, and his comments help them to Engage and Persist in the Critique process.

While Jim uses this Critique to create a positive social atmosphere, it also works to build students' understanding of key aspects of the assignment.

Through discussion, students come to recognize characteristic differences between blind and non-blind drawings. A few minutes into the Critique, Jim moves a pair of drawings that reflect this distinction well to the center of the wall and asks students to focus on them. Building on students' comments, Jim introduces the idea that while the nonblind drawings may have been more technically accurate, the blind drawings have a more direct expressive quality to them:

> Even though this might, there's a certain accuracy that's stronger here [*pointing to a nonblind drawing*]. These things are placed more in position. But there's a kind of believability here [*pointing to a blind drawing*], and that's a word that I'll use a lot throughout the year, *believability*. What makes drawing interesting is how direct your relationship is to what you're looking at, OK? And here, the relationship is in a way very direct, very honest. . . . There's not other things in the way. Like your perception of how it should look.

While students talk frequently in this Critique, Jim carefully guides the discussion to center on this key point. Thus, through a process involving the Studio Habits of Observe and Reflect (both Question and Explain, and Evaluate), Jim helps students explore a key intended lesson about the relationship between Develop Craft: Technique and Express. Jim also pushes students to see how they could use what they learned in the blind drawings in the rest of their work:

> Now obviously we don't do every drawing in the world covered up and sort of scribbling. But there's a really important lesson here in that—how can you bring some of this state of mind, in a way, to this [*pointing at a nonblind drawing*]? How can you bring this kind of . . . freedom or lack of inhibition into your work?

In this very first Critique of the year, Jim explicitly sets up the expectation that what you learn through Critique of a given assignment should be applied to your work more broadly: Jim challenges students to use the lessons from this assignment and Critique to Stretch and Explore beyond their usual habits of art-making.

As shown, Jim's Critiques help students integrate various Studio Habits of Mind. By encouraging students to Engage and Persist in the Critique, Jim fosters an iterative process in which students practice Observing and Reflecting, while they also explore the relationship between Express and Develop Craft: Technique. In addition, he encourages students to Envision how they might use what they learned to Stretch and Explore beyond their usual drawing habits.

CRITIQUING THROUGHOUT THE PROCESS: FIGURES IN EVOCATIVE SPACE PROJECT   (EXAMPLE 15.2)

Jim often uses Critiques as a way to guide a class and punctuate a working session. In this midsemester figure drawing session, students were meant to focus on the expressive potential of light and of the space between figures (Express, Develop Craft: Technique; see Examples 8.1 and 12.1). Jim has set up dramatic lighting and shows examples of professional artworks (reproductions of paintings by Hopper and Diebenkorn) that have the evocative sense of space and light that he emphasizes in the class assignment. Throughout the 3-hour class, Jim repeatedly holds short Critiques to keep students on track with this focus and also to help them make explicit what they are learning about expression.

Opening Critique

Jim begins the class with a Critique that serves as a transition from one class to the next, by focusing on high-contrast figure drawings from the previous session. Unlike the first class session that centered on getting students to talk, this quick Critique has no student discussion. A key purpose of this Critique is to get students quickly into the mind frame of working and to help them build connections between what they have done in the last session and what they will do today.

Jim notes the effectiveness of all the drawings and comments that he could really see how the students were building on their previous experiences. His praise serves both to encourage students and to reinforce the idea that assignments in the class connect to each other. With a long wooden pointer, Jim draws students' attention to different areas of each drawing as he comments on the high-contrast technique and how it helps students organize space, separate shapes, reduce a complex scene, and maintain the focus on light.

Jim's stated purpose is to get students back in the mind state of working. He tells them, "I want to put you mentally to where you were last week." Jim's comments emphasize the thought process that went into making their drawings: "This shape may have been a lighter gray or toward the lighter end of the spectrum, but you make that decision to go black or white with every gray you see and what you end up with is an abstract composition."

In this, as in all his Critiques, Jim moves beyond discussing technique while simultaneously staying grounded in the work. Here he connects the use of a particular technique (high-contrast drawing) to more expressive properties in one student's drawing:

It starts to look to me almost like some Native American design, like an Incan blanket. . . . All that is, is a drawing technique, a pretty simple technique of high-contrast drawing, looking at something ordinary in the studio, and you start to move to this whole other realm of all sorts of things that are pretty magical and unusual and really have little to do with the scene we're drawing.

Jim chooses to focus on aspects of the drawings such as expression and light that will be central to the next assignment: He will assign students to do a drawing that focuses on the expressive, evocative properties of the space between two figures. Thus, this Critique, while seemingly a reflection on completed work, prepares students mentally for the coming work session and primes them for key ideas to come.

Critique of Sketches

After students complete a couple of quick sketches of two figures, Jim gathers the class around the array of sketches on the floor for a few minutes. Though he asks students a few questions, Jim is the primary speaker in this Critique, as well. In an interview, Jim explains that the purpose of this Critique was to help students envision their final drawings from the sketches and ensure that they understood the focus of the assignment. "It was to make sure that they had the maps before the journey starts." He also uses the Critique to get students "excited about possibilities of this little assignment by seeing that emotional things are already being said in the pictures."

Jim begins by integrating Observe, Envision, Reflect: Question and Explain, and Evaluate. As he surveys the drawings, he says, "I see plans starting to form in your brains about how you are going to approach this." The group looks at and evaluates the sketches in terms of what they reveal about how students envision the final drawings.

Jim chooses two students' drawings and asks the class to compare their different approaches. One student has exaggerated the distance between the figures and another has made the figures small relative to the space in the room. After talking about the expressive aspects of the piece, Jim asks, "What's different about the choices [Student 1] made and the ones [Student 2] made?" He focuses students' attention on how the drawings treat space differently. This Critique helps students learn to observe their sketches for the purpose of envisioning a more finished drawing. Jim wants them to Reflect: Question and Explain, and to Reflect: Evaluate their sketches for what they are starting to Express, and then to see if they can Envision ways of stretching to heighten this expression.

Final Critique

After the working session, Jim holds a longer Critique that involves more student discussion. In this Critique, each student's work is carefully discussed. This Critique focuses on giving students a chance to Observe and Reflect: Question and Explain, and Evaluate what they have done in their work and to get some practice talking about work (Reflect: Question and Explain). After listening to students' general observations about the works, Jim focuses the questioning on which pieces have the strongest sense of dramatic, evocative light, a central focus of the assignment (Reflect: Evaluate). When students comment on a dramatic piece, Jim often expands on their comments. For instance, he talks about how one piece has the feel of a big movie set in which only a small area is lit up, and that area is where the action is. He ties this to a "pretty strong decision" the student has made in leaving much of the drawing empty. In this way, he models how to connect observations about Express with Develop Craft: Technique. For another student, he holds up a Hopper print for comparison of the dramatic power of light. When students comment that the drawing has an "outside feel" even though it is inside, Jim ties this observation about an expressive property to a more technical idea, showing how this effect results from how the student has highlighted multiple light sources. Again, Jim connects students' learning from practicing to Observe and

Reflect: Evaluate to the central idea of the assignment, which is to link technique and expression (Develop Craft: Technique and Express). His use of the Hopper print is intended to help students begin to connect their own art-making to other artists' work (Understand the Art World: Domain).

This Critique proceeds one-by-one through each piece, with students making observations and evaluating their own work and working process, and then listening to comments about it from Jim and the rest of the students. Suggestions for further work involve noticing an interesting aspect nascent in the work (Observe and Reflect: Evaluate) and figuring out ways it could be taken further (Envision and Stretch and Explore). For instance, Jim tells one student that she can work on hers without the models so that she can focus on heightening the contrasts. This suggestion connects to her other recent work (discussed in the opening Critique) that involved building up abstract compositions. Thus, this final Critique integrates all eight Studio Habits of Mind.

These examples of Critiques illustrate that Critiques can have a variety of structures and functions. A key strength is that they aim to help students integrate their learning and development of Studio Habits of Mind. Students are meant to learn how asking questions and explaining ideas can support evaluation of a piece, to connect their work to that produced by others in their class and throughout history, to observe how different techniques can produce different expressive effects, and to stretch beyond their usual habits to envision new possibilities for their work. Teachers can guide Critiques flexibly so that they highlight the integration of different Habits at different times. For instance, in the planning stage of a drawing, Critiques may focus more on tying Observe to Stretch and Explore and Envision. Students are meant to open up and explore a range of possibilities for their work. After the work is complete, the Critique may focus on tying Observe with Reflect: Question and Explain and Evaluate. Students are meant to figure out and describe what aspects of a work function well, which do not, and why.

A Common Language for Intellectual Growth

In *Smart Schools* (1992), David Perkins describes two components of learning experiences that educators need to address. Teachers must decide *what* students should learn and *how* to teach them. Our analysis of visual arts teaching in studio programs has revealed what we believe to be the real curriculum in arts education. The *what* is a set of studio-centered "thinking dispositions" (Perkins, Jay, & Tishman, 1993) that we call the eight Studio Habits of Mind, many of which might also be useful for students in other subject areas. We also looked at *how* studio art teachers set up instruction to teach the Studio Habits of Mind and identified three Studio Structures as emblematic of studio classes. Together, the Studio Habits of Mind and the Studio Structures make up the Studio Thinking Framework.

We have outlined the Studio Thinking Framework, not as a recipe for teaching studio classes, but rather as a set of lenses for thinking about teaching and learning in the visual arts. While we built the framework by looking closely at the practices of five high school visual arts teachers, we are beginning to see it used in diverse settings—in studio and non-arts classrooms at all grade levels, in classes for other arts disciplines, and in pre-service, in-service, and graduate level contexts. In addition, we envision its use in future research on arts learning, arts assessment, and arts teaching.

In this final chapter, we discuss some of the varied ways our five collaborating teachers and teachers who were not part of the original research but who were introduced to the framework more recently, have used these ideas in their studio classrooms, reflecting their diverse professional styles, teaching goals, and students' needs. We also consider how

the Studio Thinking Framework may "put our findings to work" in other arts and non-arts disciplines, by extending arts learning goals and strategies into a range of different disciplinary and teaching contexts. And we consider how future research may explore ways to nurture and deepen learning in arts classrooms.

USING THE STUDIO THINKING FRAMEWORK IN THE VISUAL ARTS

In 2004–2006 we extended our research to Alameda County, California, where we worked with five public school visual arts teachers, two at K–8 schools and three at high schools. When observing these art teachers as they began to use the Studio Thinking Framework, we noticed that the first moves they made with it were generally to assess their own teaching:

- What habits of mind do I tend to emphasize?
- What habits are naturally built by particular assignments?
- Which habits come up frequently in individual consults with particular students?

Once these teachers spent several months viewing their own work through the lenses of Studio Habits, they began to use them in other ways. Some supervisors used them as observation tools when they visited classrooms, to monitor the emphasis of instruction. Teachers often used them to analyze their teaching intentions and/or the standards for which their instruction was meant to aim.

Assessment is a promising area of use. Since 2003, we have been examining what the Studio Habits of Mind look like for different ages of students and at different levels of understanding. Many teachers find the habits useful as ongoing assessment when observing their students, because the habits help teachers make their intentions explicit to themselves and to their students; consider who is meeting, exceeding, or falling below their expectations; and consider how they might intervene more effectively. We are now describing "levels" within habits as well as trajectories of growth in which habits are combined as students develop greater expertise. We are currently working to develop assessment tools with clear criteria for monitoring student learning and growth over time.

USING THE STUDIO THINKING FRAMEWORK IN OTHER ARTS AND NON-ARTS DISCIPLINES

The Studio Thinking Framework emerged from observation and analysis of teaching in the visual arts. However, the dispositions we identified for teaching of the visual arts are similar in type to those required in other disciplines. It seems probable that the Studio Habits of Mind differ from Habits of Mind required in other disciplines only by emphasis (e.g., there is likely more concern with "Express" in visual arts than there is in mathematics, science, or history) and the contents and contexts in which the thinking is applied (e.g., "Understand the Art World" has counterparts in "Understand the Mathematics World" or "Understand the Music World"; "Envision" in visual art may employ mechanisms that overlap with "Envision" in science). Indeed, the Studio Structures should support constructivist teaching in any discipline in which instruction keeps disciplinary work at the center of students' learning activities. And in all classes, students should be encouraged to evaluate their own work and be able to explain their work (Reflect: Question and Explain, and Evaluate), to take risks (Stretch and Explore), to become passionate (Engage), and to stick with problems over long periods of time (Persist). Therefore, the thinking dispositions that we have identified as central to visual arts teaching may also play a prominent role in other disciplines.

In other arts disciplines (e.g., music, drama, dance), teachers have compared and contrasted the case from visual arts with teaching and learning in their own disciplines. In music, for example, one might alter "Observe" to become "Listen and Observe"; in Theater, "Observe" might become "Attend" (as suggested by Judith Contrucci, Coordinator of Visual and Performing Arts for the Cambridge, Massachusetts, public schools). In "Develop Craft: Technique," music teachers might shift the subcategory "Studio Practice" to "Rehearsal Practice." And in the Studio Structures, musicians, dancers, and theater artists might add "Rehearsal" or "Ensemble" as a fourth learning structure, since collaborative group contexts are so central in teaching in those domains. With minor alterations to accommodate such specialized aims and contexts, the Studio Thinking Framework is already guiding planning and teaching in other arts disciplines by helping teachers reflect on ways to keep making and thinking at the front of their minds as they plan and teach in their own arts disciplines.

An added benefit of the Studio Thinking Framework is that it can foster professional dialogue by helping teachers in different arts disciplines consider how it is profitable to see the "arts" as a single instructional area, the ways in which it is useful to differentiate arts disciplines one from another, and the ways in which the disciplines can enhance one another. For example, in dance, classes tend to be structured with many repetitions of very short structures, such as a 1-minute Demonstration–Lecture, followed by a 2-minute Students-at-Work session and a 30-second Critique. Some music rehearsals are similarly conducted. These anecdotal observations could be the spark that leads to rigorous research analysis of these contexts to seek patterns of instruction typical in the domain and of high-quality instruction in different learning contexts (e.g., early in the introduction of a piece, when warming up, or when approaching a performance date).

In non-arts disciplines, the benefits are similar. Too often, arts teachers feel themselves relegated to the remote edge of the conversations about reforming teaching and learning. However, with the Studio Structures defined, teachers of other disciplines can consider the benefits of adding more visuals and demonstrations to their lectures, making lectures briefer, and focusing them on information that is immediately useful for the task students are about to undertake. Coupled with using Students-at-Work sessions in their classes, non-arts teachers may find that Demonstration–Lectures provide just the opportunity they need to model ways that experts in their subject areas conduct disciplinary tasks (e.g., analyzing a primary document, designing an experiment with appropriate controls, finding an intriguing problem in mathematics and systematically working to solve it).

The Students-at-Work structure is a natural for teachers of any discipline who believe that students need to construct meaning in order to understand. Teachers can observe and intervene in ways that allow them to differentiate instruction for students, depending on their needs and challenges. The structure allows teachers to emphasize formative assessment, identifying targets of difficulty and offering "just-in-time" intervention for students as they conduct research, write, or solve problems.

Finally, Critiques are a logical addition to non-arts classrooms. When teachers make occasions for student work to be viewed and discussed publicly while it is in process, students can learn to function as a community of learners focused on developing understanding as a group. This is what goes on in the Japanese mathematics classrooms as described by Stigler and Hiebert in *The Teaching Gap* (1999), in which teachers assign a single problem, groups work to solve that problem, and then the group together discusses not the answer but the processes of problem-solving. As teachers identify and define ways to contribute usefully in Critiques, they may see the reflective conversation about learning that happens during Critiques begin to carry over to times when students return to working individually.

An additional value of the Studio Thinking Framework for non-arts teachers is the assistance it offers for interdisciplinary work. Students respond to arts experiences when they are interspersed in instruction in non-arts domains. But often, the non-arts teachers have no idea what constitutes a genuine arts experience, as opposed to a trivial use. When using arts to invite interest in a non-arts topic, the Studio Habits of Mind can guide teachers to consider artistic values that the activities might foster. And, when developing interdisciplinary units among a group of teachers, having the Studio Habits available makes it easier to identify overlapping concerns between the non-arts disciplines and the arts. Such overlaps seem a promising area of exploration for rigorous interdisciplinary studies and/or research about effectiveness in interdisciplinary curricula.

USING THE STUDIO THINKING FRAMEWORK BEYOND THE CLASSROOM

The Studio Thinking Framework could also be used in future research to demonstrate best practices that promote learning. Using this tool, researchers will be able to describe and contrast classroom practices more precisely. Ultimately, research should be able to determine which particular variations result in higher levels of student learning in particular contexts. For now, though, such conclusions are premature. What we present here is a description of the range of patterns that we observed in five classrooms. By reflecting on these examples, we believe that teachers can become more aware of and better able to refine their own teaching practices.

In addition, we see the Studio Thinking Framework as a tool to promote professional dialogue across local, district, state, and university contexts and across arts disciplines. And, in politically charged atmospheres of accountability and tight budgets, the Studio Habits of Mind can help explain and justify programs to parents, administrators, and groups who control resource allocation to schools.

Our framework is now starting to be used by diverse groups of teachers, in visual arts, other arts, and non-arts disciplines, and we are just beginning to learn how its usefulness may extend beyond refining classroom instruction. We hope that you, readers of this book, will be alert to ways that the Studio Thinking Framework supports your efforts to teach rigorously, both within and beyond the classroom context. When you put the framework to use, please, let us hear from you!

Project Examples

School and Teacher	Project Name	Example Number
The Boston Arts Academy		
BETH BALLIRO	African Pottery	4.1, 12.2
	Imaginary Creatures	8.2, 10.1
	Inventing Colors	5.1, 7.1, 13.1
	Secret Ritual Vessels	14.2
	Sketching in Clay	11.1
KATHLEEN MARSH	Egg Drop	12.7
	Creating Hat and Vest	14.4
	Mounting the Show	12.5
	Making Puppets	6.2
	Self-Portraits in Colored Pencil	5.2, 10.3
MICKEY TELEMAQUE	Using the Viewfinder	9.1
Walnut Hill School		
JASON GREEN	Centering on the Wheel	5.4, 14.1
	Ceramic Sets	12.3, 13.2
	Coil Sculpture	4.2, 10.2, 12.6
	Repeating Units	11.2
	Tile Project	6.1, 7.2
JIM WOODSIDE	Abstraction	14.3
	Contour Drawing	15.1
	Cubism	12.4
	Figures in Evocative Space	8.1, 12.1, 15.2
	Light and Boxes	4.3, 5.3, 9.2

Conducting the Research

Research is only as trustworthy as the methods by which it is conducted. This appendix describes the methods we used to develop the Studio Thinking Framework to make transparent the empirical processes we employed in our research design.

SETTINGS AND SUBJECTS

Over the 2001–2002 school year, we filmed 38 classes in five classrooms at two high schools that focus on the arts, the Boston Arts Academy and the Walnut Hill School. The five teachers all were practicing artists. The three teachers at the Boston Arts Academy are teachers licensed by the state of Massachusetts, and all five teachers have Master's degrees, either M.F.A.s or M.Eds or both. Students at the Boston Arts Academy are proportionally representative of the demographic profile of the Boston area in socioeconomic status. Students at Walnut Hill are an international group including local suburban and urban students and students from across the United States and from abroad, with a concentration of Korean students. Students at Walnut Hill are mainly middle or upper-middle class with some students receiving full scholarship. At both schools students are admitted by portfolio review and/or on the basis of admissions tasks and interviews. Students who are admitted showed interest and promise in the visual arts, but few have highly developed levels of technical skills upon admission.

DATA COLLECTION AND FIRST-LEVEL ANALYSIS

We documented classes that ranged from 1.5 to 3 hours in length; twenty-two classes at the Boston Arts Academy and sixteen classes at Walnut Hill. Nine sessions were 3-hour, 9th-grade classes at the Boston Arts Academy; seven were 1.5-hour 9th-grade classes at the Boston Arts Academy; sixteen were 3-hour mixed 9th- through 12th-grade introductory classes at Walnut Hill; and six were 3-hour 12th-grade classes at the Boston Arts Academy. This yielded a total of 103.5 hours of classroom observation. Data included videotapes with audio shot by our project videographer that focused on the teacher, field notes by a second researcher–observer, and memos written by the observing researcher immediately following each observation. Videos captured teachers talking to students but not conversations between students.

After each filming, we created video clips of events in the classroom that we wanted to learn more about, based on our review of the memo and on debriefing conversations between the videographer and observer. We wrote a standard interview protocol that we revised for each class to suit the particular data, and we followed up with an audiotaped interview of the teacher about a week after the filming. During interviews one researcher viewed clips together with the teacher and probed what was going on. Additional data were collected in the form of photographs of student work and curriculum documents and/or program descriptions.

DATA ANALYSIS

Videos and audiotapes of the interviews were transcribed. Analysis triangulated video and audio transcripts, videos, photos of student work and curriculum documents, and field notes and memos. Iteratively, we looked for patterns of interactions and uses of time and space, both within each teacher's classes and across all five teachers. This resulted in identification and then definition of the Studio Structures, which are based on characteristics observed across the teachers.

We then segmented transcripts of the documented classes into categories for each Studio Structure. Next, we reviewed the Students-at-Work segments of four classes we selected randomly as code-development cases, in order to develop categories of what we saw being taught. We looked for patterns in the transcripts and then developed "native" concepts that described how each teacher talked about his or her intentions for student learning. Next, our research team collapsed the teachers' personal concepts into fewer categories, resulting in 11 "codes" for intended learning and a code we called "other." Through iterative comparisons across codes within the four code-development

classes, our team of five researchers created a coding manual with examples from the transcripts that we used to guide the next phase of analysis.

At this point, we randomly selected and assigned about 35% of the remaining classes (12) to three members of our research team, two of whom coded each class. During this process, we continued to bring examples that confused us to our meetings to refine our codebook. When analysis of the 12 classes was complete, we tested the reliability across coders and found that it was strong (between 0.7 and 0.9). We then randomly divided the remaining 22 classes among the three coders so that each coder analyzed seven or eight classes.

As we began discussing our preliminary findings with others in the field, we eliminated the "other" category and, in three cases, combined two codes (Technique and Studio Practice were combined into "Develop Craft"; Question and Explain and Evaluate were combined into "Reflect"; and Domain and Collaborate were combined into "Understand the Art World: Domain and Communities"). The resulting eight categories of "what" art teachers intend to teach became the eight Studio Habits of Mind presented in the chapters in Part II.

References

Amabile, T. M. (1996). *Creativity in context.* Boulder, CO: Westview Press.

Bostrom, M. (2003). *Fulfilling the promise of No Child Left Behind. A meta-analysis of attitudes towards public education.* Public Knowledge LLC. http://www.keepartsinschools. org/Preview/Research/Materials/NoChildLeftBehind-MetaAnalysis.pdf

Burger, K., & Winner, E. (2000). Instruction in visual art: Can it help children learn to read? *Journal of Aesthetic Education, 34*(3–4), 277–294.

Butzlaff, R. (2000). Can music be used to teach reading? *Journal of Aesthetic Education, 34*(3–4), 167–178.

Csikszentmihalyi, M. (1990). *Flow: The psychology of optimal experience.* New York: Harper and Row.

Deasy, R., & Fulbright, H. (January 24, 2001). Commentary: The arts impact learning. *Education Week, 20*(19), 34.

Efland, A. (1976). The school art style: A functional analysis. *Studies in Art Education, 17*(2), 37–44.

Efland, A. (1983). School art and its social origins. *Studies in Art Education, 24*(3), 149–157.

Eisner, E. (2002). *The arts and the creation of mind.* New Haven, CT: Yale University Press.

Ellis, A. (2003, June). *Valuing culture.* Paper presented at conference entitled Valuing Culture, National Theatre Studio, London. Available at http://www.demos.co.uk/ catalogue/valuingculturespeeches/

Fiske, E. (Ed.). (1999). *Champions of change: The impact of the arts on learning.* Washington, DC: Arts Education Partnership and President's Committee on the Arts and Humanities.

Harland, J., Kinder, K., Haynes, J., & Schagen, I. (1998). *The effects and effectiveness of arts education in schools.* Interim Report 1. London: National Foundation for Educational Research.

Hetland, L. (2000a). Listening to music enhances spatial–temporal reasoning: Evidence for the "Mozart effect." *Journal of Aesthetic Education, 34*(3–4), 105–148.

Hetland, L. (2000b). Learning to make music enhances spatial reasoning. *Journal of Aesthetic Education, 34*(3–4), 179–238.

Keinanen, M., Hetland, L., & Winner, E. (2000). Teaching cognitive skill through dance: Evidence for near but not far transfer. *Journal of Aesthetic Education, 34* (3–4), 295–306.

Lampert, M. (2003). *Teaching problems and the problems of teaching.* New Haven, CT: Yale University Press.

McCarthy, K., Ondaatje, E. H., Zakaras, L., & Brooks, A. (2004). *Gifts of the muse: Reframing the debate about the benefits of the arts.* Santa Monica, CA: RAND Corporation.

Murfee, E. (1995). *Eloquent evidence: Arts at the core of learning. Report by the President's Committee on the Arts and the Humanities.* Washington, DC: National Assembly of State Arts Agencies.

Perkins, D. (2001). Embracing Babel: The prospects of instrumental uses of the arts for education. In E. Winner & L. Hetland (Eds.), *Beyond the soundbite: Arts education and academic outcomes* (pp. 117–124). Los Angeles: J. Paul Getty Trust.

Perkins, D. N. (1992). *Smart schools: From training memories to educating minds.* New York: Free Press.

Perkins, D. N., Jay, E., & Tishman, S. (1993). Beyond abilities: A dispositional theory of thinking. *Merrill-Palmer Quarterly, 39*(1), 1–21.

Podlozny, A. (2000). Strengthening verbal skills through the use of classroom drama: A clear link. *Journal of Aesthetic Education, 34*(3–4), 91–104.

Salomon, G., & Perkins, D. N. (1989). Rocky roads to transfer: Rethinking mechanisms of a neglected phenomenon. *Educational Psychologist, 24*(2), 113–142.

Stevenson, H. (1994). *The learning gap: Why our schools are failing and what we can learn from Japanese and Chinese education.* New York: Simon & Schuster.

Stigler, J. W., & Hiebert, J. (1999). *The teaching gap: Best ideas from the world's teachers for improving education in the classroom.* New York: Free Press.

Tishman, S., Jay, E., & Perkins, D. N. (1993). Teaching thinking dispositions: From transmission to enculturation. *Theory Into Practice, 32*, 147–153.

Tishman, S., Perkins, D. N., & Jay, E. (1995). *The thinking classroom: Learning and teaching in a culture of thinking.* Boston: Allyn & Bacon.

Vaughn, K. (2000). Music and mathematics: Modest support for the oft-claimed relationship. *Journal of Aesthetic Education, 34*(3–4), 149–166.

Vaughn, K., & Winner, E. (2000). SAT scores of students who study the arts: What we can and cannot conclude about the association. *Journal of Aesthetic Education, 34*(3–4), 77–89.

Vygotsky, L. (1978). *Mind in society: The development of higher psychological processes.* Cambridge, MA: Harvard University Press.

Vygotsky, L. (1984). *Thought and language.* Cambridge, MA: MIT Press.

Winner. E., & Cooper, M. (2000). Mute those claims: No evidence (yet) for a causal link between arts study and academic achievement. *Journal of Aesthetic Education, 34*(3–4), 11–75.

Winner, E., & Hetland, L. (Eds.). (2000). The arts and academic achievement: What the evidence shows. *Journal of Aesthetic Education, 34*(3–4), 3–307.

Winner, E., & Simmons, S. (Eds.). (1992). *Arts PROPEL: A handbook for visual arts.* Cambridge, MA: Project Zero at the Harvard Graduate School of Education and Educational Testing Service.

Index

About the Authors

Lois Hetland is an Associate Professor of Art Education at Massachusetts College of Art and a Research Associate at Project Zero, Harvard Graduate School of Education. She received her Ed.D. from the Harvard Graduate School of Education in 2000. Trained in music and visual arts and formerly an elementary and middle school classroom teacher for 17 years, her work as a developmental psychologist focuses on learning, understanding, and teaching in the arts and other disciplines. Her most recent prior research was a series of meta-analytic reviews for Reviewing Education and the Arts Project (REAP), 1997–2000, including two reviews of music's effects on spatial reasoning. That project's work was published in an invited special issue of the *Journal of Aesthetic Education*, which she co-edited. REAP has been widely discussed in *Beyond the Soundbite: Arts Education and Academic Outcomes* (co-editor, 2001), in a dedicated issue of the *Arts Education Policy Review* (May/June, 2001), in commentary on National Public Radio, and in articles in *The New York Times*, *Education Week*, and numerous other newspapers and magazines. Lois was Co-Principal Investigator of Project Zero's subcontract to the Alameda County Office of Education's VALUES Project (Visual Arts Learning for Understanding Education in Schools) and is Principal Investigator of the current subcontract focused on the spread of that pilot, both funded by the United States Department of Education. She is also a Co-Principal Investigator of the Qualities of Quality Project, funded by the Wallace Foundation, has served as the Education Chair of Project Zero's annual summer institute from 1996 to 2005, has taught an online course on professional development for teachers on Harvard's WIDE platform (Widescale Interactive Development for Educators) from 2000 to 2005, and consults nationally and internationally on arts and on teaching and learning for understanding. She authored the staff development guide to Project Zero's video series, *Educating for Understanding*, co-edited two volumes based on Project Zero's institutes, and is co-authoring *The Dimensions of Understanding Guide*.

Ellen Winner is a Professor of Psychology at Boston College and a Senior Research Associate at Project Zero, Harvard Graduate School of Education. She received her Ph.D. in Developmental Psychology from Harvard University in 1978. Her research focuses on learning and cognition in the arts in typical and gifted children. She is the author of more than 100 articles and three books: *Invented Worlds: The Psychology of the Arts*, *The Point of Words: Children's Understanding of Metaphor and Irony,* and *Gifted Children: Myths and Realities*, which has been translated into eight languages and was awarded the Alpha Sigma Nu National Jesuit Book Award in Science. She received the Rudolf Arnheim Award for Outstanding Research by a Senior Scholar in Psychology and the Arts from the American Psychological Association. She is a Fellow of the American Psychological Association (Division 10, Psychology and the Arts) and of the International Association of Empirical Aesthetics.

Shirley Veenema is an instructor in visual arts at Phillips Academy, in Andover, Massachusetts, and is a researcher at Harvard Project Zero. She served as project manager and videographer of this project. Originally focused on printmaking and mixed media drawing, much of her current work as an artist is also in media. Her recent media work includes five videos for the show, *Dangerous Curves: Art of the Guitar*, at The Museum of Fine Arts, Boston, and a series of interactive documentaries funded by the Cultural Landscape Foundation.

Kimberly M. Sheridan is an assistant professor in the College of Education and Human Development and the College of Visual and Performing Arts at George Mason University. She received her Ed.D. from the Harvard Graduate School of Education in 2006. While in graduate school she received a Spencer Research Training Grant, and her first year of work on this project was as a Spencer Research Fellow. Her dissertation research examines taste judgments and the development of taste, looking in particular at how film fans of all ages develop taste for films. Her previous work at Project Zero was on the GoodWork Project, which looks at the intersection of excellence and ethics in a range of disciplines and professions. She is trained in the visual arts and previously received a Fulbright fellowship to study contemporary East African art.